THEORY AND REALITY OF INTERNATIO

To Maria,
my daughter

Theory and Reality of International Politics

HANS MOURITZEN

Ashgate

Aldershot • Brookfield USA • Singapore • Sydney

Published by
Ashgate Publishing Ltd
Gower House
Croft Road
Aldershot
Hants GU11 3HR
England

Ashgate Publishing Company
Old Post Road
Brookfield
Vermont 05036
USA

British Library Cataloguing in Publication Data
Mouritzen, Hans, 1952-
    Theory and reality of international politics
    1. World politics 2. International relations
    I. Title
    327

Library of Congress Cataloging-in-Publication Data
Mouritzen. Hans.
    Theory and reality of international politics / Hans Mouritzen.
        p. cm.
    Includes bibliographical references and index.
    ISBN 1-85521-993-X (hardbound)
        1. International relations--Philosophy. 2. Geopolitics.
    I. Title.
    JZ1251.M68   1998
    327.1'01--dc21   97-39120
                                                CIP

ISBN 1 85521 993 X

Printed and bound by Athenaeum Press, Ltd.,
Gateshead, Tyne & Wear.

Contents

List of Figures   *vii*
List of Abbreviations   *viii*
Preface   *ix*

1   Introduction   **1**

2   The Argument   **5**
Levels of Explanation   5
International Politics: Anarchy and States' Non-Mobility   7
Spatial Heterogeneity vs. Temporal Homogeneity   11
Why State the Obvious?   13
Modifications and Counter-Modifications   14

3   IR Theory: A Critical Evaluation   **19**
Literature on Explanatory Levels   19
'Comparative Foreign Policy' and Small State Research   22
The Theory of Kenneth Waltz   24
From Bipolarity to Post-Bipolarity   28

**4   The Preferred Mode of Explanation:
     A Further Presentation**   **31**
Explanatory Logic and Level   31
Salient Environment and Polarity   33
Environment Polarities: Illustrations   36
European Heterogeneities 1989-94: From the Hague to Kiev   38

5   Testing Theories   **43**
Tension between the Strong and the Strategy of the Weak   43
Balancing vs. Bandwagoning: Testing Balance-of-Power Theory   50
Nordic Engagements vis à vis the Baltic Countries:
     A Geopolitical Approach   64

6   Salient Environment and Domestic Explanatory Factors:
     The Nature of the Interplay   **81**
     Levels of Explanation: Complementarism vs. Supplementarism   81
     The House on Fire   82
     External Danger/Internal Cohesion-Centralization   84
     Non-Mobility Revisited   90
     Control, Relax, Guide   93
     Inertia and Foreign Policy Lessons   94
     The Role of Internal Factors in Theory-Building   95

7   Two Illustrations of Interplay   **97**
     Learning within Geopolitical Parameters: Alliance Policy
        from Helsinki to Warsaw   97
     European Integration and National Bandwagoning 1989-94:
        Facing a Pole of Attraction   103

8   The Role of International Organizations   **113**
     IGOs: The Control-Relax Mechanism Reapplied   113
     IGOs as State Instruments   126
     Control-Relax and Theories of European Integration   130

9   Theory and Reality of International Politics   **137**
     Conclusions   137
     Critical Rationalism and its Realism   141
     Complementarism vs. Supplementarism Revisited   151
     IR Schools: Why Bother?   153

Bibliography   **159**

Index   **169**

List of Figures

Fig. 2.1 Basic types of systems from the viewpoint of explanatory level   7

Fig. 3.1 External pressures on the national actor: Waltz' view and that of the present book   27

Fig. 4.1 Power wanes with distance from home (A,B)   34

Fig. 4.2 Systemic vs. environment polarities in an international system   35

Fig. 4.3 Events/regions as sources of major challenges   39

Fig. 4.4 Three constellations in unipolar Europe 1989-94   41

Fig. 5.1 Balancing vs. bandwagoning in Finnish, Swedish and Danish responses to the Soviet disintegration   62

Fig. 5.2 Distances to the Soviet Union/Russia and the Baltic countries from each of the Nordic countries   66

Fig. 5.3 Nordic engagements for the Baltic cause 1989-91 as expected from the twin distance model   69

Fig. 5.4 Nordic engagements for the Baltic cause post-1991 as expected from the twin distance model   73

Fig. 6.1 Three models of interplay between external and internal foreign policy determinants (adapted from Goldmann)   83

Fig. 6.2 The control-relax model during 'relax': the external and the permitted internal factors can be added   92

Fig. 7.1 National adaptation to (regional) unipolar integration: a general model   104

Fig. 8.1 A control-relax model for IGOs: state control in high and low politics   119

Fig. 9.1 Supplementarism and complementarism   151

List of Abbreviations

CAP	Common Agricultural Policy
CFSP	Common Foreign and Security Policy
EC	European Community
ECJ	European Court of Justice
EPC	European Political Cooperation
EU	European Union
FCMA	Treaty of Friendship, Cooperation and Mutual Assistance
IFOR	Implementation Force (NATO in Bosnia)
IGO	International Governmental Organization
IM	Internal Market
INGO	International Non-governmental Organization
IR	The International Relations Discipline
NATO	North Atlantic Treaty Organization
OSCE	Organization of Security and Cooperation in Europe
SEA	Single European Act
SOP	Standard Operating Procedure
UN	United Nations
WAPA	Warsaw Pact

Preface

International politics is like a formal dinner, whose guests are seated according to a pre-planned table arrangement. Each guest is obliged to the pleasant or unpleasant company of two or three other guests sitting next, irrespective of his or her preferences; apart from the most dominating personalities, the general noise prevents conversation from being conducted on a broader scale. Correspondingly, the major units in international politics ('nation-states' until further notice) chiefly interact with states in their geographical neighbourhood, even though certain units have a wider action space than others. Units being bullied by a neighbouring great power do not have the option of escape.

In most of international relations (IR) theory-building, however, it is tacitly assumed that the units of international politics are mobile. In other words, international politics is seen rather like a reception, whose guests can circle freely among each other. This has led to much mistaken theory-building.

The main thesis of this book is that nation-states' mutual non-mobility constitutes a fundamental property of international politics, on a par with its much debated anarchy (the absence of an international government). This may sound banal, but the combination of 'banal' and not-so-banal assumptions adds up to wide-ranging implications for how theories of international politics should be built.

The present book has not been intended as an IR textbook. However, its rather polemic style arguing its own original view may in fact be a fruitful way of addressing some of the IR 'great debates' for graduate students, mainly. The book is not structured around IR schools (realism, utopianism, liberalism, institutionalism, etc.); they give too little constructive guidance for theory-building, although still dominating in teaching and scholarly debates. The most important contribution of inquiry is neither accurate description, nor predictive usefulness. Rather, it is explanation of something puzzling us; a 'theory' is only a theory, if it can explain (and preferably explain much by little). That makes it sensible to structure a book like the present one around explanation – in case of international politics and the behaviour of its major units (foreign policy). Levels of explanation and their interrelationships offer the book's structure.

I am grateful to several students and colleagues at the University of Copenhagen, at COPRI (The Copenhagen Peace Research Institute) and at DUPI (The Danish Institute of International Affairs), my current employer, for listening patiently to my non-mobility argument ever since 1978, as I first read Kenneth Waltz's presentation of his theory in *Handbook of Political Science*. Some suspected that I was joking, others took it seriously; I fully respect both types of reactions.

DUPI has provided skillful technical assistance in the preparation of the manuscript. Apart from technical assistance, Harvard graduate student Christian Sparrevohn has read and commented constructively upon each and every chapter, on details as well as on basic points. As always, however, I carry responsibility for the book's content, including any errors or misjudgements. Finally, I thank my family for their patience and endurance.

HM
Copenhagen
August 1997

1 Introduction

Molecules in a gas or consumers in a market are mobile; there is no specific and stable environment for each unit. After some drifting around in various segments and corners of the system, the 'average environment' of each unit can be equated with the system, it forms part of: the gas or the market. In this sense all units face the same environment. By contrast, nation-states in international politics are mutually non-mobile; this is an implicit, but fundamental property of international politics on a par with its anarchy. Non-mobility means that each state faces a specific and stable salient environment rather than the international system as a whole. Since power and incentive wane with distance, it follows that each state's salient environment will have significant explanatory power in relation to its behaviour (foreign policy). However, most of the academic international relations (IR) discipline proceeds, as if states were mobile like floating vessels in the sea with no specific environment. It has been discussed to the brink of boredom in IR, whether 'systemic' or 'domestic' factors can explain foreign policy and international politics, but states' salient environment is apparently forgotten. It is puzzling why this repression has taken place in the IR community unlike among historians or journalists, for instance. One reason is probably that theoretical constructs have been uncritically imported from branches of science studying systems of mobile units (economics and cybernetics, for instance). Also, IR as a relatively young discipline desiring scientific respectability may have felt that its comprehensive object of study – the international system – should be somehow 'important' and therefore carry a reasonable explanatory power of its own. In this way, however, it has become a straitjacket for theoretical development.

Post-bipolarity has made regional and local power structures more important at the expense of an overall systemic structure. This may explain the renewed interest in geo-politics, for instance. It is too superficial to say, however, that the current systemic polarity requires other theories than did bipolarity. As I shall argue, post-bipolarity makes certain enduring peculiarities of international politics more *visible* than they were during bipolarity, but the point is that they have been there all the time.

International organizations or other non-state actors may be allowed an influence of their own in certain areas, but the state remains in ultimate control. Likewise, internal factors may sometimes be permitted an influence on foreign policy, but states' salient environment is ascribed explanatory primacy in this book. The conception of international politics offered here invites a bottom-up instead of a systemic top-down perspective, but without falling prey to reductionism (explaining international politics from internal factors, mainly). Explanation of state behaviour should be made primarily on the basis of states' respective salient environments – that tend to vary considerably from state to state.

All this is about segments of reality: I assume reality existing independently from our language and theories about it. This disentanglement of theory and reality makes a confrontation between the two a meaningful enterprise; through this, it should be possible to learn that one theory is better than another. We avoid relativism, i.e. of the form 'you can have your paradigm, theories, and assumptions, and we can have ours'. 'Theory' is understood here in a non-puristic sense as a set of interrelated assertions about reality, from which empirically testable expectations can be derived. The assertions have common underlying reasonings with their own independent justification, explaining *why* we should believe them to be true. 'Theoretical construct' is a wider concept, covering not only theories, proper, but also less developed models, hypotheses, and pre-theories. A 'pre-theory' is a construct saying, typically: 'if your object of explanation is such and such, look to a certain *class* of factors for a good explanation'. It also provides reasons, why we should look in that particular direction. In this book, two pre-theories are established: one about the importance of units' salient environment at the expense of systemic explanation for understanding international politics, and one indicating the nature of the interplay between salient environment and internal explanatory factors. Within the 'action space' provided by these pre-theories, specific theories are formulated and tested.

Chapter 2 presents the non-mobility argument, along with some modifications to it (keeping the door ajar for systemic explanation under special circumstances). Chapter 3 surveys the IR literature on explanatory levels and demonstrates the shading of the environment level taking place here. The systemic theory of Kenneth Waltz as well as the reductionist approaches of 'comparative foreign policy' and small state theory are critiziced on the basis of the non-mobility argument, essentially. Chapter 4 turns to a further presentation of the preferred explanatory logic and level. The notion of environment polarity instead of the usual systemic polarity is introduced and illustrated. In chapter 5, three different theories rooted in the salient environment are formulated and tested: one about tension between the strong and activity of the weak, another about balance-of-power between the strong and bandwagoning of the weak, and a third one labelled a 'twin distance model'. In empirical terms, it explains the five Nordic countries' respective Baltic engagements on the basis of their geographical distances from the Soviet Union/Russia and from the Baltic Sea region. In chapters 6 and 7, we climb down the level ladder – only to conclude that the salient environment should be ascribed primacy in relation to internal explanatory factors. Two illustrations of external/internal interplay are offered: 1) alliance policy in the Baltic Sea rim space, in which foreign policy heritages are added to basic geopolitical factors, and 2) bandwagoning in the face of a pole of attraction (the European Union), where all kinds of domestic factors are added to (but subsidiary to) the European polarity restrictions. Even though a state-centric conception of international politics prevails in this book, chapter 8 investigates theoretically and empirically the precise nature of this state-centrism in relation to international governmental organizations (IGOs) and the EU. The latter entity necessitates that we relate to prevalent theories of regional integration. Methodology should preferably be post-hoc, i.e. reflection on some presented theoretical construct rather than an apriori credo. This unavoidably lends it a certain pharisaical flavour that the reader will have to endure (chapter 9). Whereas discussion of IR school belongingness is hardly fruitful for constructive purposes, the philosophy of science school of critical rationalism has served as a guideline for the present book. That is made explicit in this final chapter.

2 The Argument

The global international system has two fundamental properties: it is non-hierarchic (some would say anarchic), and its major units are mutually non-mobile. The properties are fundamental in the sense of being non-reducible to more basic ones. Only the former of these two properties has been subject to attention in IR theory, IR 'great debates', or IR textbooks. I shall argue here that this is a devastating mistake: the combination of the two properties has farreaching consequences for the kind of theories and explanations that can be fruitfully applied within the field. So whereas non-mobility in itself is a rather self-evident fact (probably the reason why it is overlooked), its *implications* are wideranging; they are actually at odds with mainstream developments within IR[1].

Analogously to consequences deduced from the traditional assumption of international anarchy (e.g. the security dilemma, the prevalence of national security interests), the implications derived here are necessarily of a somewhat imprecise nature. They pertain to relative potencies of levels of explanation in international politics.

Levels of Explanation

I shall operate here with 'level of explanation' instead of the vague notion of 'level of analysis' – being responsible for much confusion (one reason being that 'analysis' may also encompass description and prediction apart from explanation). An explanation is the answer to a 'why-question'; the object of explanation is what puzzles us and 'requires' an explanation. The source of explanation is what explains this object. *Level* of explanation is the locus of this source[2].

---

1   I use 'IR' (international relations) here as encompassing foreign policy theorizing. Foreign policy being an essential element of international politics, any disciplinary exclusion of this branch of theorizing would be hair-splitting. Pace Waltz (chapter 3), one cannot have a good theory of international politics/relations without a reasonable theory of the behaviour of its major units.
2   On levels of explanation vs. objects of explanation, cf. Mouritzen 1980. I first brought forward the argument of 'spatial fixity' in this article (pp. 172, 180 note 15), albeit in passing. It led to little or no reaction. Explanation can also be classified according to its logic (causal vs. finalistic) or its temporal dimension (synchronic vs. diachronic). Only the latter, however, is relevant to the argument made here.

International politics is understood here as the interaction of two or more international units. In other words, negotiations between Croatia and Slovenia is as much international politics as the Cuban missile crisis, and also reactive behaviour is a form of interaction. The immediate object of explanation in the below discussion is foreign policy, that is the content of the external behaviour of nation-states[3]. Since nation-states are the major units of international politics, this object of explanation is difficult to disentangle from international politics as here understood.

Let us turn to the specific levels of explanation to be discussed. At the systemic level, international politics – typically its distribution of power – is viewed from a bird's eye perspective; a camera snap-shot is taken from above in order to elucidate the backcloth of nation-state behaviour. Of course, we may zoom in at a particular region, as in subsystemic analyses. The salient environment level, by contrast, entails something qualitatively different: the world – its polarity, not least – is viewed from the bottom-up perspective of the specific nation-state, whose behavior we wish to explain. The camera has been lowered to the nation-state capital in question and turned upside down. 'Environment polarity' or 'bottom up polarity' may sound like contradictions in terms, because we are used to thinking of polarity from a systemic perspective. Of course, only a segment of the world can be caught by the camera lense from this particular frog perspective. The camera analogy is crucial: I am not talking about particular decision-makers' *perceptions* of the salient environment; that belongs to a separate level of explanation: the decision-making level. I am talking about the salient environment of a nation-state, as it can be construed by analysts as objectively as possible, and no less objectively than systemic attributes. For instance, whereas the overall system may count as unipolar, because there is only one superpower, the salient environment of state 'X' may simultaneously be tripolar, as in addition to the superpower two local great powers have roughly the same ability to project power in relation to 'X'. Finally, there is the level of units' domestic factors: foreign policy is sought explained on the basis of party competition, the activities of domestic pressure groups, public opinion, etc.

The principle of level classification used here is the step-wise abandoning of simplifying assumptions: at the salient environment level, we abandon the systemic level assumption that all units face one and the same environment (the system); at the domestic factors' level, we abandon the assumption that

---

3   In other words not foreign policy process; that may play a role as a *source* of explanation, of course.

units (nation-states) react similarly irrespective of subgroup competition; and at the decision-making level, we abandon the assumption that governments react similarly, irrespective of idiosyncratic factors, bureaucratic factors, or factors in the very decision-making process. What is being classified, hence, is what an explanation emphasizes as interesting or peculiar (carrying explanatory weight); however, any explanation is simultaneously based on assumptions pertaining to other levels, whether they be explicitly formulated or tacitly assumed.

International Politics: Anarchy and States' Non-Mobility

An 'international system' is defined here as a system with no relevant political environment. Through this definition, it should also encompass certain historic systems with less than global extent. Let us briefly put such a system into perspective in relation to other types of systems. In the four-fold table in fig. 2.1, we have the system's basic ordering principle along one dimension (hierarchy vs. non-hierarchy) and the mutual mobility of its units along the other dimension.

Fig. 2.1 Basic types of systems from the viewpoint of explanatory level

	Hierarchic ordering	Non-hierarchic ordering (incl. anarchic)
Units mobile	I. *A military system*	III. *A market place*
Units non-mobile	II. *A human body (or other organism)*	IV. *An international system*

What levels of theorizing are likely to be fruitful for each of these types of systems? In particular, what are the prospects for systemic theorizing – that explains units' behavior by pointing to attributes/developments of the system as a whole[4]? If the units are mobile, then each unit will face a persistently shifting environment. It will probably seek towards a beneficial environment,

---

4 As should appear, 'systemic explanation' is here used in a broader sense than that established by Kenneth Waltz – cf. pp. 25-6.

but so will all other units. This entails continuous adjustments of position on behalf of all units. Therefore, a unit's 'average' environment, when considered over a reasonable[5] time-span, is the system as a whole – not any particular segment of it. If the units are non-mobile, by contrast[6], each unit has a stable neighbourhood, consisting of a few geographically adjacent units and their mutual relationships. The environment in its essential traits typically keeps constant for whole 'eras', only to be broken off by the dissolution of neighbouring units or other dramatic events. The unit is bound to face this salient environment whether it likes it or not; it cannot drift away so as to acquaint itself with some new neighbours. The challenges it seeks or faces are likely to originate mostly from this specific environment, since power and incentive wane with distance, other things being equal; this pertains both to its own power/incentive and that of others[7].

When it comes to explanation and theorizing regarding the unit's behavior, then, the crucial factors are more likely to be found in this *salient environment* than being attributes/developments of the system as a whole. Conversely, if the units are mobile and therefore facing no particular environment, the latter type of explanation is likely to be much more relevant (quite disregarding units' internal attrubutes, of course, that may be relevant both for mobile and non-mobile units). One can say, therefore, that units' non-mobility has introduced a *cleavage between unit and system* – each unit's salient environment. From the viewpoint of accounting for units' behaviour, this entails an extra explanatory level in its own right.

As should be obvious, non-mobility is different from territoriality or spatiality as such. Also movement takes place in space. Non-mobility, however, entails that certain spatial relations are frozen and made into almost permanent conditions. Also non-spatial distances may be frozen, as ideological distances between political parties in a multi-party system (e.g. Sjöblom 1968). Such parties are relatively non-mobile in relation to each other, since credibility concerns prevent them from switching place on an ideological left-to-right scale. This means that each party has a salient environment; its main concern is competition with its neighbouring parties to the right and left for voters, not least. This salient environment may be more important than attributes of the party-system as a whole for the explanation of its behaviour.

---

5   'Reasonable' meaning here the time it takes to circle around in most corners of the system.

6   As should appear, I operate with full mobility and non-mobility, solely. One might imagine semi-mobile units that are able to move in certain segments of a system. That, however, would only obscure the point I wish to make.

7   Regarding the power aspect of this, cf. Spykman 1942 p. 448 or Boulding 1962, ch. 12. Cf. also O'Sullivan 1986, ch. 5. This will be further developed in chapter 4 below.

I shall only say a few words about the second dimension, as this has been subject to abundant and persistent IR attention. Obviously, a hierarchic order entails a more coherent and consciously coordinated system than an anarchic one. The actor at the apex – embodying the system – is likely to have a good deal of control over units' behaviour and will therefore provide a natural locus of explanation regarding the system's functioning. This represents *one* type of systemic explanation, albeit not the only one. A non-hierarchic order is likely to be more heterogeneous from the viewpoint of such overall explanation; as will be argued, some types of structures are likely to keep a looser grip on units' behaviour than others – thereby leaving more room for the role of local explanatory factors.

These two reasonings shall now be combined and applied to the illustrations mentioned in the categories of fig. 2.1:

I) a hierarchic system with mobile units: a military system is a paradigm example of a hierarchic system. Moreover, its units are mobile, both in the most literal sense as soldiers in the field and when it comes to officers' career patterns, requiring typically the geographical moving from one military unit to another within relatively short time-intervals. It is actually the 'system's' strategy to safeguard that the officers do not get time to establish too strong local loyalties (a salient environment); their overall dependence and gratitude must be vis à vis the army/navy/air force as such. A rotation system is one means to secure this. Should one wish to *explain* the activities of a military sub-unit, its leadership (the system) is likely to carry much more weight than its equals/subordinates.

II) a hierarchic system with mutually non-mobile units: a human being, or any organism for that matter, is an extremely coordinated unit by virtue of the central nervous system – to an extent that even a military organization would envy. But in contrast to the latter, its sub-units are mutually non-mobile: they are located in certain pre-determined positions that enable the organism to function adequately. This means that each sub-unit has a certain salient environment. Therefore, a fist punching a person, for instance, could theoretically be explained by the adjacent arm's movement (which in turn could be further explained after the same principle). However, unless we are physiologists, we would prefer an explanation stressing the punching person's *reasons* for doing this, his state of mind, etc. At the level of the organism, this is a systemic explanation.

III) a non-hierarchic system with mobile units: a market place is, by definition, non-hierarchic. Still, a systemic explanation (e.g. Adam Smith's 'unseen hand') is appropriate, when it comes to the explanation of consumers' and suppliers' behaviour, as well as the price level. This is because of the units' mobility: a consumer can move freely to a new supplier, should he or she be dissatisfied with the conditions offered by the current supplier. Consumers as well as suppliers respond to one and the same set of systemic market conditions; there is no salient environment for each of them.

IV) a non-hierarchic system with non-mobile units: an international system fulfills both of these criteria. Its by far most important units, the nation-states, are mutually non-mobile. Small powers being subject to bullying from a neighbouring great power cannot 'escape' to a more benign environment. Of course, exile governments may exist during extreme conditions; but their raison d'être is the hope that they will once be able to return to their geographical home-base. It might be objected that the long reach characterizing certain great powers could make it out for mobility. This has something for it (cf. the modifications below) but still, the difference between a mobile unit and a non-mobile one with long reach is that the latter has a home-base. A fixed target being easier to hit than a moving one entails that it has higher strategic vulnerability. It *will* have an extra-salient environment, after all[8]. It seems that we have to go back in history to systems of nomadic tribes in order to find international systems of mutually mobile units.

From the two sets of reasoning above, it follows that *an international system is the system-type that should be the **least** suited to systemic explanation among those four considered above.* Each nation-state has its own salient environment, and there is no strong central coordinating mechanism – as in the example of the human body – that can overrule this and make (one type of) systemic explanation worth while, after all. Systemic explanation may still be relevant under certain special conditions; but in *comparison* to these other system-types, the international system is not hospitable to systemic explanation.

It should appear from the above argument that non-mobility is a more fundamental property than spatiality. Together with the other assumptions (anarchy, power/incentive waning with distance), however, non-mobility

---

8   This is not to deny, of course, that other powers' salient enviroments are being affected by this long reach.

makes space essential in international politics – and thereby location for each unit in it.

Spatial Heterogeneity vs. Temporal Homogeneity

Heterogeneity rather than homogeneity is likely to prevail, as we compare the situations of various units in this kind of system. Exposing identical units to identical stimuli will often lead to different reactions, given the different characteristics of units' salient environments. By contrast, the picture is one of homogeneity and stability, if we follow one and the same unit over time. Of course, salient environments are transformed in the wake of major wars or state dissolutions – as when states fell apart in Central and Eastern Europe post-1989. This created new neighbours for others, evidently. Still, the *general* picture is that salient environments – and thereby foreign policy orientations – keep relatively constant for whole eras like 1949-89 in Europe. They are stable – but mutually different. Consider for instance the stable Cold War security policies of Finland (Soviet dependent neutrality), Sweden (neutral), Norway (low profile NATO allied), Denmark (low profile NATO allied), and the Netherlands (NATO allied). Using the level classification used above, the considerable difference between these policies can hardly be explained systemically (the bipolarity of the international system, the states' ranks in the power hierarchy); nor can differences in domestic factors or decision-making factors serve as adequate explanations (the countries being roughly similar). The states simply had different salient environments, being differently *located* in the bipolar structure on a permanent basis. To put it bluntly, the static factor of distance to the Red Army was decisive: the shorter the distance, the more cautious posture was upheld (presupposing the Soviet Union as a status quo power pole, cf. chapter 7).

Most of the variance in international politics is found synchronically between units, rather than diachronically for individual units. The pattern is the reverse in a system of mobile units such as an arena of dodgems in an amusement park. The situation of each dodgem changes dramatically all the time; it has no specific and stable environment. Considered over a reasonable time-span, all dodgems have made roughly the same set of standard experiences: frontal collision, being hit by another dodgem from behind, from the side, etc. Should we account for the typical driving of the dodgems, the 'systemic level' would be close at hand: the number of dodgems in the arena and the latter's size, the rules of driving, etc. As these are common to all dodgems, their driving is unlikely to differ much. However, *should* we explain the peculiar driving of a specific dodgem, this would require a knowledge of 'unit attributes': mechanical deficiences of the dodgem in question, or a particular aggressiveness of its driver, for instance. There is no unit/system cleavage and thereby no salient environment for each unit as in international politics.

Each unit in an (anarchic) system of mobile units should be alert all the time, as it must be prepared on short notice to face the most threatening unit in the system. 'Security' will be a permanent concern. By contrast, non-mobility as in international politics entails that *some* units are dangerously located (e.g. neighbouring a threatening unit), whereas others enjoy a more peaceful location[9]. Be it one way or the other, units will have quite stable and orderly environments that are relatively easy to grasp – if not at the outset of an era then to an increasing extent over time. Stable salient environments invite custom and habit at all levels; one gets used to a certain external constellation and the challenges that it poses. Certain SOPs (standard operating procedures) are developed, not only in bureaucracies but also among top decision-makers. Essentially the same parliamentary or other foreign policy debates are repeated over and over again, decade after decade. The same goes for a gradually more specific bureaucratic code language.

Non-mobility entails that national stereotypes may be applied to units in the neighbourhood, notably: 'big brother complexes' (at the popular level, notably) or the 'hereditary enemy.' By being unable to circle freely around, nations are forced to remain in enduring rivalries, be they symmetric dyads with a 'hereditary enemy' or in asymmetric dyads, in which at least the weaker party would probably prefer to drift away, if possible. One victorious party cannot cut and run with its conquest (e.g. Germany with Elsass Lothringen in 1871); the defeated party remains in the neighbourhood, probably preparing for revenge (Alsace Lorraine being recaptured by France 1918). Such pendulum effects may go on for centuries[10]. On the other hand, the positive side of these interlocked relationships is that the nations in questions may learn to live decently with each other in a kind of maturing dyads (as in the example), simply because it is their common interest under non-mobility. They may learn it the hard way by going through military conflict; but it is also likely that the very anticipation of such conflict entails mutual restraint and caution.

---

9   On this heterogeneity as criticism of the IR schools of neo-realism and neo-liberal institutionalism, cf. chapter 9.

10   For a rich survey of 'enduring rivalries', cf. Goertz (1994) ch. 10. Cf. also, for instance, Stein (1996).

The kind of spontaneity and sincerity that can be afforded vis à vis faraway nation-states can be dangerous in the salient environment; after all, one has to be capable of living relatively decently together in the future with neighbours that one is locked to almost by fate (the 'shadow of the future' in game theory, cf. below).

Why State the Obvious?

Why should the salient environment deserve to be emphasized in this way, one might ask? Any sane historian, journalist, or political analyst wishing to explain foreign policy knows what I have stated here – and follows it in his or her actual explanatory practice[11]. He/she will typically find it too obvious to state – and rightly so. But it is far from obvious in an IR context. For the purpose of theory-building, models have often been borrowed from branches of science covering the three *other* types of systems described above. For instance, Waltz's systemic/structural theory of international politics has been explicitly inspired by micro-economic theory (being intended for category III above); Kaplan's and others' systems theories/structural functionalism have been (partly) borrowed from biology/General Systems Theory (being intended for category II) and/or cybernetics (the science of goal-seeking mechanisms, being intended for category I and II). In principle, there is nothing objectionable in borrowing inspiration from whatever field of inquiry that one wishes; *the fallacy consists in importing models that are tailored to systems with no system/unit cleavage and applying them to a kind of system, where this cleavage is crucial.* This does in no way entail that international politics should not be 'exposed' to nomothetic theorizing; it only means that theorizing has to pay due respect to the peculiarity of the international system named the system/unit cleavage and, consequently, ascribe a crucial role to salient environment factors in the explanation of unit behaviour. Formal modelling like game theory may be relevant with the proper assumptions – like the 'shadow of the future' (Oye, 1985). In iterated games as opposed to single-play games, the prospects of continued interaction with the *same* players entail that immediate gains from unilateral defection does not pay off in the long run. Mutually non-mobile units are subject to the 'shadow of the future', obviously.

---

11   Supplementing, often, their salient environment explanations with unit-level explanations (internal factors, factors in the decision-making process, etc.)

It has required an economist (engaged in inter-disciplinary research) to formulate theoretically one of the fundamental *peculiarities* of international politics/conflict:

> Yet another difference between international conflict and the competition of firms is the much greater importance of geographical boundaries in international relations. The firm competes in a market area where boundaries are shifting and ill defined and where effort is spread over the whole area rather than being concentrated at the boundary (Boulding, 1962, p. 264).

Modifications and Counter-Modifications

Under special conditions, systemic explanation of unit behaviour ('foreign policy') may after all be worth while. I shall now discuss some modifications to the argument made so far. Firstly, it makes a difference, whether we are dealing with *pole* or *non-pole powers*, the pole powers being those who constitute the global power structure at stake (the US and the Soviet Union in the bipolar era). Systemic explanation is in one sense more natural regarding the behaviour of the pole powers. As these are identical to the systemic poles, they are not subject to as deep unit/system cleavages that the non-pole powers are. They *are* (part of) the structure in a direct sense; their salient environment consists mostly of other pole powers or perhaps even the whole systemic structure apart from themselves. This means that their behaviour is both significantly conditioned by the overall structure (as well as by other factors) – and that they also deliver important feedback to it. However, this modification has its limitations during multipolarity, in particular, where even pole powers may be located differently in the structure and therefore be subject to different salient environments (cf. fig. 4.2). This brings us to the next modification.

Secondly, overall-structural polarities do actually vary among each other according to the (lack of) causal power, they command over units' behaviour. The *least* powerless is probably bipolarity. The structure's grip pertains primarily, of course, to the two poles, because they constitute symmetrically each others' salient environments as mirror images. Thereby they avoid a unit/system cleavage. The structure's grip also pertains to varying degrees to other powers being subject to bipolar overlay. This difference between polarity types has been vividly illustrated by the breakdown of bipolarity in Europe (cf. pp. 38-42).

A third modification to the general argument is that more far-reaching weapon-types together with improved means of transportation and communication lead to increased *international interdependence*,other things being equal. This entails a reduction in the importance of geographical distance (Boulding, 1962, ch.13) and thereby environment incongruities. By its very nature, high interdependence makes it more reasonable to operate with systemic conditions proper, i.e. conditions being *common* to all or most states – in general or within a certain sector, thereby blurring the distinction between 'system-as-such' and unit salient environment.

International monetary instability, for instance, may serve as a systemic explanation of the devaluation of individual states' currency, or an international economic crisis may explain trade or monetary restrictions of individual states. By contrast, states trading overwhelmingly with their particular neighbours (due to less advanced means of transportation, e.g.) entails that their trade policy be best explained by economic conditions and policy among states in their particular neighbourhood.

Ecological degradation has been emphasized as an aspect of increased international interdependence. It is questionable, however, what that means in the present context. Global heating due to increased carbon dioxide in the atmoshpere is a challenge common to all, of course. Still, most types of degradation are spatially conditioned: the (risk of) nuclear outlets from reactors or sulphur from the chimneys of not-so-distant countries, for instance. That means that incentives for bilateral cooperation or conflict regarding problems of this type are significant in the neighbourhood – or wane with distance, to use the general formulation in this book.

Many of the Cold War strategic weapon-systems (ICBM, for instance) limited the importance of spatiality somewhat. Some nation-states could, in principle, inflict 'unacceptable damage' to others, irrespective of distance. Still, this modification should not be overstated, due to the continued prevalence and credibility of conventional weapon-types. After all, the important Soviet Allies were those that were within reach of the Red Army tanks after 1945. Any glance at a map revealed that the Soviet Allies in Europe were not arbitrarily spread out.

The stressing of interdependence and its technological and other background-factors as a set of *catalysts* for the structure's grip on the units has been made by, e.g., the Sprouts (1956), Mouritzen (1980), Ruggie (1986), Keohane & Nye (1987), Christensen & Snyder (1990), Buzan et.al.(1993), and Christensen (1993), albeit under different labels. Introducing these catalysts is tantamount to saying that the structure's grip is in no way self-evident; it is, in other words, a criticism of the alleged universal applicability of overall-structural explanation[12]. To take the notion of 'interaction capacity' (Buzan et.al., 1993, pp. 66-80) as an example: for most of history (until the last few centuries), the interaction capacity of the overall international system ('the level of transportation, communication and organisation capability') has been so modest that it has prevented a 'structural logic' from working across the system as a whole; the civilizations of Europe, the Middle East, India and China have been largely self-contained. During the last centuries, however, the system has reached a level of interaction capacity sufficient to support the structural logic across the system as a whole (p. 77). The subsystems (regions) are believed to 'remain only as a shadow' during these conditions. The position taken here is that I fully accept the fruitfulness of 'interaction capacity' as a descriptive-comparative instrument for international systems over the centuries. The notion can account for the very *existence* of an overall international system today and for the most recent centuries. But it keeps silent about the *explanatory* qualities of this system that we are interested in here. With few remarkable exceptions the rule is that the explanatory power of the overall system has been modest or negligible. Even if the interaction capacity of today's system makes *possible* extensive interactions between, say, the Netherlands and Japan, the level of interactions between the Netherlands and Germany is much higher. One need not consult trade or tourist statistics to be aware of that. Even a perfectly interconnected international system does not overrule the fact that one is primarily connected to one's neighbours.

A fourth point to emphasize – already hinted – is that systemic vocabulary may be useful for *descriptive/comparative* purposes. When dealing with a number of historic international systems (Rosecrance 1963), it is useful from a comparative point of view to label them as, e.g., unipolar, bipolar, multipolar, or use other systemic vocabulary. Moreover, as a prelude to environment explanation of unit behaviour, it may be natural briefly to describe the properties of the overall international system. This is, of course, perfectly legitimate, as long as one does not mistake it for explanation. In Singer's view (1961), description rather than explanation was actually the main purpose of his systemic level of analysis.

These modifications notwithstanding, salient environment should have explanatory primacy at the expense of the overall system regarding unit

---

12   These catalysts can also, in themselves, be given a system-wide interpretation. In order to keep them apart from overall structural explanation, they are sometimes labeled 'systemic, non-structural' factors.

behaviour, given the peculiarities of international politics compared to other types of system. Systemic explanation should be the exception rather than the rule, relevant only under special conditions. General theory-building, therefore, should not be anchored at the level of the international system.

3 IR Theory: A Critical Evaluation

Literature on Explanatory Levels

Before evaluating two significant traditions of IR research in relation to the argument that has been made in chapter 2, I shall provide a brief survey of the abundant IR 'level of analysis' literature[1]. Several authors have discussed levels of analysis, either in independent articles or as byproducts of major empirical research efforts. Where necessary, I shall 'translate' the levels at stake to our levels of explanation in this book.

Waltz (1959) operates with a systemic level ('image'), internal factors' level and a 'human' level for the purpose of explaining international conflict. Singer's classical article (1961) distinguishes between a 'systemic' and a broad 'subsystemic' level of analysis; Rosenau (1966) deals with five 'sets of variables' (= levels here) in his widely cited and applied 'pre-theory': apart from the systemic variables and the societal variables (internal factors), there is a governmental set, a role set, and an idiosyncratic set of variables (further developed by Väyrynen (1972), section 2.1). Spanier (1972) sees a systemic level, a level of internal factors and a decision-making level. Hollis and Smith (1990 pp. 8-9) suggest four levels: international system, nation state, bureaucracy and individual. A 'survey of scientific findings' (McGowan, Shapiro, 1973) includes 'other nations' policies' (belonging to the salient environment level here) as one out of thirteen sets of variables; however, 'we see that the research employing others' policies is quite limited' (p. 159). The rest of the environment level is merged with systemic variables in a rather confusing way. The influential volume 'Why Nations Act' (East et.al. eds., 1978) classifies previous theorizing on foreign policy behaviour in seven different categories, according to their explanatory level. But the salient environment level gets a stepmotherly treatment, to say the least: one expects to find it in the chapter on the foreign policy 'situation' (ch.9), but this turns

---

1   I shall not distinguish sharply between authors with a systemic object of explanation and those aiming towards the explanation of foreign policy, solely. The reasons are that several 'levelists' are vague on this point and the fact that some of them see their levels as applicable in relation to both objects of explanation.

out in fact to deal with decision-makers' perceptions/definition of the situation – i.e. the decision-making level as here conceived[2]. Both Allison (1972) and Jervis (1976) do actually delineate levels that coincide with the environment level as here understood (although the rational-actor assumption of Allison's 'model I' is not a requirement, as we saw). On the other hand, the message of both books is that rivalling (lower) levels provide better explanations; hence, the role of the environment level is that of a backcloth to allegedly more fruitful levels[3]. Brecher (1972), using the notion of an 'operational environment' (inspired by the Sprouts, 1956) – in its external aspects including a global level, a subordinate one and a level of bilateral relations – obviously encompasses what we are dealing with here. Still, the psychological environment (the decision-making level) is regarded as 'the motor force of state behaviour' (p. 542). Wilkenfeld et.al.'s (1980) 'inter-state' level (as distinct from a 'global' one) comes rather close to the salient environment level as here conceived. In their investigation of relative potencies, the result was that 'the inter-state realm is the key predictor of foreign policy behavior...'(p. 170); the global and the societal clusters were second and third in this respect (p. 191)[4]. Most & Starr (1989) and Goertz (1994 p. 103) both lay a distance to the relative potency discussion at stake here; 'both the environmental/ structural level and the decision-making/ choice level are required for a full description and explanation of international relations phenomena' (Most & Starr 1989, p. 23). It is obvious from the *actual* analyses in both of these works that the

---

2   Interestingly, the very existence of an environment level (labeled 'external variables') is actually recognized in this volume; reference is made to such attributes as number of alliances to which a nation belongs, number of intergovernmental organizations of which it is a member and distance in air miles from the Soviet Union. It is then carefully argued, why this level is *different* from the level of national attributes (p. 125), and why it is *different* from the systemic level (pp. 146-47). Strangely enough, however, it is not treated on its own terms in this intendedly exhaustive volume.

3   For some strange reason, Jervis includes 'a state's geographical position' (1976, p. 21) among 'domestic determinants'; in my level conception, it forms the backbone of the salient environment. Hoffmann's concept of the 'national situation' is 'made up altogether of its internal features – what, in an individual, would be called heredity and character – and of its position in the world' (1970, pp. 77-78); it embraces, in other words, both the environment level and that of internal factors. Wolfers (1962 p. 40) distinguishes between environmental and 'predispositional' (here: internal) determinants of state behaviour. The environment level is represented in Mouritzen (1980).

4   Strangely enough, Wilkenfeld et.al. (1980, p. 78) subsume a unit's number of IGO memberships and borders under the global factor (p. 78); this makes their findings all the more supportive of a salient environment perspective as here conceived.

environment level is ascribed a significant explanatory role at the expense of the systemic level[5]; however, they never make the tension between the two explicit, but instead lump them together as in the above citation (cf. also Goertz 1994, p. 5). The preferred level in security complex analysis (Buzan 1991) is subsystemic/regional, a sub-level to the systemic one. Even though the camera zooms in at a particular region, it is still a top-down perspective: the picture is taken from above rather than from the frog perspective of a specific nation-state (cf. illustrations in chapter 4).

On the basis of the non-mobility argument made above, we should expect the salient environment level to be superior to the systemic level for explanation of unit behavior. As should appear already from this survey, however, this is far from the case as seen by IR. In fact, rather few recognize the salient environment as an explanatory level in its own right. In particular, relatively few distinguish between a systemic and an environment level. It seems as if the systemic level tends to shade the latter level. One mechanism among others that may be responsible for this is the IR discipline's desire to have a single overarching focus. It seems to be a (mostly unstated) assumption in scholarly debates that since the discipline exists (i.e. with all its outward symbols of scientific respectability), there must certainly exist a corresponding entity – 'the international system' – with reasonable explanatory power. This is, of course, an invalid argument. Apparently, it is not so intellectually appealing 'only' to ascribe the international system the descriptive-comparative value that was recognized above[6]. Secondly, it seems to be tempting to slip quickly from the operational environment to the psychological level. The descriptive truism that the environment must be *perceived* by decision-makers in order to affect unit behavior (or that 'decisions are made by men, not by environments', Brecher, 1972, p. 556) may divert attention from the operational

---

5   Goertz's notion of a 'barrier' to nation-state action is an example of this (1994, ch. 6). As he admits, 'the often-used language of 'structure' is in many ways not the best one, in fact the barrier may be only one state as in the case of USSR-Eastern Europe' (p. 95). On the related concept of 'bastion' and the building of bastions vs. others, cf. Mouritzen (1988).

6   As observed by Harf et.al. (1974), those who have studied the significance of systemic variables empirically '...have been primarily concerned with the effect of one systemic property upon another...Few scholars, if any, have focused on the relationship of systemic properties to the foreign policy behavior of nations' (pp. 237-8). The former type of analyses – mostly descriptive (Singer 1961, cf.above) – seem to have conferred a popularity upon the concept of 'system' in the widespread *level rhetoric* that it by no means deserves in relation to the explanation of unit behavior.

level and its relative explanatory potency in its own right[7]. Perception or decision-making factors have only explanatory potency, if there is something peculiar about them.

I shall now concentrate on the accomplishments of two major IR traditions: one whose ultimate dependent variable is nation-state behaviour ('comparative foreign policy', CFP, and related research) and one in which the understanding of such behaviour is an integral part of the explanation/ prediction of systemic outcomes (Waltz's theory of international politics).

'Comparative Foreign Policy' and Small State Research

Among several efforts aiming towards general theory of nation-states' external behavior, James Rosenau's socalled 'pre-theory' of foreign policy was by far the one with the greatest organizing effect on subsequent research. As suggested by Hermann and Peacock (1987, p. 24), one reason for this was its manageable agenda being suitable for large-scale comparative studies (as in CFP, 'Comparative Foreign Policy'). The pre-theory (Rosenau 1966) was the first to raise the relative potency question within a systematic framework. Various 'source variables' – systemic, governmental, domestic, role, idiosyncratic – were ascribed relative explanatory potencies in relation to foreign policy, according to which *type of state* was at stake. Eight 'genotypes' could be deduced from a typology of nation-states based on size (small/large), economic development (rich/poor) and political accountability (open/closed). They were intended as parameters: for instance, the small/rich/open type of states would have role variables as the most important source of behavior and systemic variables as no. 2.

One point of criticism from the standpoint of the argument made here is that the environment is overshadowed by the systemic level among the source variables by being lumped together with it. This makes the framework blind to diverging salient environments. Moreover, pure unit attributes (size, economic development and political accountability) function as parameter. This would suit a sea of vessels floating around, each representing a 'genotype'. Each type would float in its own characteristic way and experience persistently

---

7   Still, Brecher suggests a general proposition about long-term state behavior: 'the psychological environment of a decision-making group in foreign policy is in large measure a product or mirror of the operational environment'(1972 p. 556). If true, this should entail a modest relative potency to the psychological environment, to say the least. Brecher does not draw this inference, though (cf. the motor force analogy cited above).

new environments. A methodological weakness of the pre-theory is that the *reasonings* underlying the primacy conferred upon the three genotype variables or the ranking of the source variables are not made explicit (except for note 45). Such explicitness would have reduced the inductivism of much subsequent CFP research and improved the opportunities of learning from false predictions.

A CFP sub-category – even if sociologically unrelated to it – is 'small state' or 'weak state' theorizing, seeking to account for foreign policy on the basis of size, solely[8]. As frequently pointed out by critics and small state theorists themselves, it has proven impossible to identify any uniform pattern of behavior characterizing 'small states' (let alone agree on a definition of this concept). Recall, for instance, the behavioral heterogeneity along the Cold War continuum of small states stretching from Finland to the Netherlands mentioned in chapter 2. Even if small state theorists usually pay due respect to the salient environments of their empirical targets, this is not included in their theorizing; the unit attribute of size is their 'master variable'.

As pointed out by Rummel (1969, p. 612), 'foreign conflict behavior is not internally derived...It is a relational phenomenon depending on the degree of economic, social and political similarity between nations, the geographic distance between them and their power parity'. This and other deficiencies of the pre-theory were observed and to some extent corrected by Rosenau in subsequent writings. In the socalled 'extended pre-theory' (Rosenau and Hoggard, 1974; Rosenau and Ramsay, 1980 [1975]), 'external' variables were separated from systemic variables as here conceived (although no big deal was made out of it; cf. Rosenau and Hoggard, 1974, footnote 3). Moreover, three relational (non-unit) variables were made the backbones of a typology of dyads: distance between the dyadic parties (remote/ proximate), their societal homogeneity (similar/ dissimilar) and their (power) equality (equal/unequal). Like the original unit-based genotype, this relational one was conceived as a parameter for the understanding of the functioning of the source-variables. Obviously, it is suited to a system of mutually non-mobile units consisting of innumerable and relatively stable dyads subject to the 'shadow of the future', cf. chapter 2. But of course, dyads are only *one* component of salient environments and not necessarily the most basic one (as conceded by Rosenau and Hoggard, 1974, fn.6).

The pre-theoretical improvement never managed to catch the attention of the original pre-theory. Internal factors strongly prevailed in CFP – both before and after the pre-theoretical extension. As vividly illustrated by Chittick

---

8   See Christmas-Møller, 1983, for a survey and discussion.

and Jenkins (1976 p. 284), only 2 out of 60 ICFP papers[9] dealt explicitly (but not exclusively) with external factors. The peculiarity of international politics as here conceived has been largely ignored in CFP, as the studies '...either employ variables at the level of the state which do not allow them to measure important aspects of the environment or they employ variables at the level of the system as a whole' (Chittick and Jenkins, 1976, p. 284).

Still, conceptual efforts stressing the non-systemic, external realm were represented by the articles by Harf et.al (1974), Harf et.al. (1976) and Chittick and Jenkins (1976). The study by Wilkenfeld et.al. (1980) can be seen as an empirical counterpart to these articles, giving full credit to the 'inter-state' explanatory level.

The adaptation tradition, likewise initiated by Rosenau (1967), has lived a life of its own mostly outside the US (e.g. Petersen 1977, Smith 1981, Mouritzen 1988, Mouritzen et.al. 1996), and its intellectual adherence to CFP has from the outset been highly questionable and is today negligible. Its common denominator is an interest in the 'vertical' balance between a unit and its environment, between 'what is desired at home with what is possible abroad' (Rosenau 1967 p. 983), thereby reformulating Hanrieder's concepts of (external) compatibility and (domestic) consensus (Hanrieder 1967). Its preferred explanatory level has increasingly become environment attributes.

The extensive inter-disciplinary literature on conflict/ war, with classic geopolitical roots (e.g. Spykman 1942), is predominantly environmental in its explanatory emphasis (the same level as conflict/ war itself). This is undoubtedly so by virtue of the 'reality touch' springing from its strong empirical-inductive orientation. The drawback of this orientation, however, is a marked lack of theoretical cumulation (cf. the evaluation by Most & Starr 1989). Nonetheless, the synthesis developed by these authors through the concepts of (external) 'opportunity' and (domestic) 'willingness' points to an interesting, though unrecognized, convergence with Hanrieder (1967; compatibility and consensus) and adaptation theory[10].

The Theory of Kenneth Waltz

I shall now relate the discussion of the unit/system cleavage in international

---

9   ICFP – the Inter-University Comparative Foreign Policy Project – was an institutionalized research effort within 'comparative foreign policy'.

10   As in much IR, however, no cumulation takes place for the simple reason that no reference is made.

politics to the theory of international politics by Kenneth Waltz. The fact that his is a *full-fledged theory* entails that we can proceed a significant step further than above: we can see, what awareness/neglect of the unit/system cleavage entails for the possibilities of providing successful predictions.

Waltz's theory, by necessity, must also be one of foreign policy (cf. Mouritzen 1997a pp. 76-77, Tellis 1996 pp. 76-8 and, most extensively, Elman 1996), in spite of his frequent disclaimers (e.g. Waltz, 1979, p. 72). In view of Waltz's own epistemology (pp. 147-9, 153, 157 below), he cannot meaningfully establish a theory of systemic outcomes (war and stability) without pre-supposing a theory of the units in this very system. Even if the system may be more than the 'sum of the parts', it is *also* the parts and their behavior. Of course, Waltz can only explain such behavior in very rough outline, given his crude assumptions about these units. But a would-be theory based on domestic factors, solely (that Waltz refers to as a 'foreign policy theory'), would be equally crude. Additionally, Waltz consistently uses the double formulation 'behavior and outcome' about his object of explanation, and several followers of Waltz have actually turned their major interest towards unit behavior (e.g. Posen 1984, Walt 1987, Christensen & Snyder 1990, or Labs 1992).

Waltz sets out to explain units' behaviour and systemic outcome from 'structural' attributes of the international system as a whole. Following the methodological principle of parsimony – i.e. seeking to explain much by little – Waltz includes as little as possible in this 'structure': its only variable element is the distribution of capabilities across units – in practice the number of great powers (multipolarity, bipolarity, etc.)

More fundamental than this polarity, however, is the almost gravitational law of international politics, irrespective of the number of poles: that of balance-of-power. In an anarchic system of units that wish to survive and prosper (Waltz 1979 pp. 121, 125-26), the units will seek to (counter-) balance a winner (an aggressor) rather than bandwagon (i.e. join it or support it). This is seldom out of concern for the system, but is deduced by Waltz from pure self-interest (i.e. to prevent a hegemon from emerging, and because joining an aggressor is dangerous). Non-pole powers do not deviate from the powerful ones:

> Secondary states, if they are free to choose, flock to the weaker side; for it is the stronger side that threatens them. On the weaker side, they are both more appreciated and safer, provided, of course, that the coalition they join achieves enough defensive or deterrent strength to dissuade adversaries from attacking (ibid. p. 127).

The *means* of balancing varies according to the distribution of capabilities –

so that 'behavior and outcome' will be widely different during different polarities. But balancing as such is seen as a universal behavioural trait of anarchic (= international) systems.

The empirical record for 'secondary states' seems to be mixed regarding balancing vs. bandwagoning, partly due to conceptual differences (cf. the discussion and survey of literature, pp. 51-7, 97-103). The point is, however, that states balance/bandwagon in the face of power conditions in their respective salient environments. 'The stronger side' systemically in the above citation may very well be the weaker side there and vice versa. Waltz's theory does not take into account that power wanes with distance.

In spite of the above citation concerning 'secondary states', Waltz might reply here that his prime concern is not with what weak powers are doing, because his theory is ultimately about systemic outcomes. And as weak powers contribute so little to the total outcome, prediction failure regarding their behaviour is not essential. Let us, therefore, enlarge the scale and consider Western Europe after World War II (Walt, 1988, p. 280). The prediction of balance of power theory would be that these countries would join the weaker of the two superpowers – i.e. the Soviet Union. But exactly the opposite happened, formalized with the creation of NATO. Or consider a major power like China. According to balance of power theory, China should support the weaker of the two superpowers – which was the Soviet Union even as her capability culminated. But what happened? We got instead the Sino-American rapprochement during the 1970s and 1980s. The reason was, of course, that the Soviet Union (allied with Vietnam) was the major power in China's salient environment, not least given her extensive border with that country. In combination with deterioration of Sino-Soviet relations, the faraway superpower became the natural ally – analogously to the example of Western Europe in the wake of WW II. A consideration of the *local* balance of power – i.e. the trend in the US/Soviet balance of power in China's salient environment – would have avoided the prediction failure of balance of power theory.

A way of thinking closely related to that of local balances of power is balance of threat theory, developed by Stephen Walt (1987, 1988). States' alliance behaviour is determined by the (im)balance of threat facing them – not the *one* balance of capabilities in the overall international system. This theory can account not only for the two cases of prediction failure mentioned above, but also for the cases where balance of power apparently succeeds. Stephen Walt describes his theory as a 'refinement' of that of Waltz. My point is that it amounts to nothing less than a revolution; there is no international system left in Stephen Walt's thinking with any explanatory power. A balance of threat (or a local balance of power for that matter) is meaningful in relation to a certain location, only (with a specific salient environment); Waltz's balance of power, by contrast, is a systemic mechanism.

What is the underlying reason, then, why balance of threat theory supersedes balance of power theory? Because, in my view, the former theory in contrast to the latter (unknowingly) pays due respect to the unit/system cleavage – in virtue of its locational orientation. Waltz's theory does not:

> The environment is produced by the actions and interactions of states, but that environment then appears like a market in a competitive economy, as a force that no state acting alone can control (Waltz, 1975, p. 41).

Already in 'Man, the State and War, it was said that

> ...the implication of the third image is, however, that the freedom of choice of any one state is limited by the actions of all others [i.e. not 'some others'] (1959, p. 204).

In other words, all states face one and the same 'market', one and the same 'whole' (cf. fig. 3.1).[11] Like consumers in a (perfect) market or molecules in a gas, states are tacitly assumed to be freely mobile, so that environment

Fig. 3.1 External pressures on the national actor: Waltz' view and that of the present book

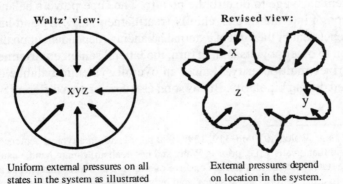

Waltz' view:

xyz

Uniform external pressures on all states in the system as illustrated by Waltz (1979, p. 100)

Revised view:

x

z

y

External pressures depend on location in the system.

---

11   Waltz (1979 pp. 82-127) often talks about a state's 'position in the system'; that, however, never means geographical location, but instead its rank in the international power pyramid (strong/weak).

heterogeneities are non-existent (ibid.) Waltz obviously disagrees in the peculiarity of the international system that was argued in chapter 2:

> The logic of anarchy obtains whether the system is composed of tribes, nations, oligopolistic firms or street gangs (Waltz 1990, p. 37).

With such a parsimonious theory as the one established by Waltz, one has to accept that deviations between theory-derived expectations and empirical observations are more the rule than the exception; nobody is more aware of this than Waltz himself. Often, factors at the decision-making level are referred to as the source of deviation (e.g. 'Bismarck's diplomatic virtuosity'); at other times, internal factors are seen as 'responsible': governmental forms, economic systems, social institutions, or political ideologies. But the point is that for Waltz, the alternative to the systemic level – and, hence, his theory – is *always* the unit level dealing with attributes *of* units. It is never situations *around* units[12].

From Bipolarity to Post-Bipolarity

Two modifications supporting systemic explanation – bipolarity and focus on the system's pole powers – are relevant in the case of Waltz' theory. That is the reason why it sounded convincing after all, when applied to its contemporary world. Focusing on the two superpowers – that not only constituted bipolarity but also formed each others' salient environments – meant that there was no unit/system cleavage to disturb the picture. The superpowers balanced each other through internal means, chiefly (rearmament, e.g.) By and large, they were independent of the kind of external balancing (dependent upon diplomacy in relation to other powers and, in turn, the latters' salient environments) that characterizes multipolarity. Hence, an overall systemic balance of power functioned during bipolarity. But as soon as we move to a different polarity[13],

---

12   Cf., e.g., Waltz, 1979 pp. 119, 139; 1990 pp. 31, 36. In a typical sentence (1990, p. 34), it is said that „realists [i.e. prior to Waltz and neo-realism] cannot handle causation at a level above states because they fail to conceive of structure as a force that shapes and shoves the units". In other words, „above states" can only mean structure. It seems likely from the survey of level literature that the Waltzian dichotomy of the form 'if not system, then unit; if not unit, then system' has affected a whole generation of IR theorists, and it still prevails as much as ever (Elman 1996, pp. 37, 41, and note 82, just to mention a single example).

13   An impression of the reduced predictive powers of Waltz's theory during multipolarity (compared to bipolarity) is provided by Christensen & Snyder, 1990, and Snyder & Jervis, eds., 1993.

or we move beyond the superpowers in the bipolar system, the systemic balance of power is replaced by numerous local balances of power/threat that tend to blur – or even negate – the fragile effects, if any, of the systemic polarity. The overall structure having lost its grip on units' behavior, it likewise loses its 'control' over most systemic outcomes. The theory's sole area of fruitful application (where it *seems* to function) is the special case of superpowers during bipolarity[14].

It is crucial to remember, however, that whereas post-bipolarity has made the unit/system cleavage more *visible,* it has been there all the time. It is too superficial just to say that multipolarity requires other theories than bipolarity. Post-bipolarity will make us aware, hopefully, of the seemingly enduring peculiarities of the international system in relation to other types of systems.

---

14 Another fruitful application of the theory should be *regional* bipolar symmetries, outside Waltz's concern, as in 'security complex analysis', cf. Buzan 1991. A unit/subsystem cleavage will generally be easier to overcome than a unit/system cleavage. Still, even neighbouring nation-states within one and the same regional sub-system will often have widely different salient environments.

4 The Preferred Mode of Explanation: A Further Presentation

Explanatory Logic and Level

The main thesis of this book is that the peculiarity of international politics – non-hierarchic with mutually non-mobile units – makes the salient environment a level in its own right and a more potent level than the systemic one for explaining unit behavior. This necessitates a further presentation of the logic and substance of explanation from salient environment.

As stated by Karl Popper in his criticism of holism and historicism,

> Psychologism [the doctrine that...social laws must ultimately be reducible to psychological laws, since the events of social life...must be the outcome of motives springing from the minds of individual men] is, I believe, correct only in so far as it insists upon what may be called 'methodological individualism' as opposed to 'methodological collectivism'...But the belief that the choice of such an individualistic method implies the choice of a psychological method is mistaken...if motives (or any other psychological or behaviourist concepts) are to be used in the explanation, then they must be supplemented by a reference to the general situation, and especially to the environment. In the case of human actions, this environment is very largely of a social nature... (Popper, 1966, vol.2, pp. 91, 90).

In other words, there is something 'between' holism (explaining from system attributes) and reductionism (explaining from unit attributes as in psychologism). In fact, there are two different sets of theories in-between: non-holist structural theories like micro-economic theory (that has served as Waltz's inspiration, cf.chapter 3), but also the Popperian or Weberian situational (here: salient environment) level of theorizing (cf., e.g., Popper, 1961 p. 152; Stinchcombe, 1968, ch.5; Lukes, 1973, p. 129; Watkins, 1973, p. 88). No matter what level preferences one happens to have, it is undeniable that there exists a level of theorizing that accounts for unit behavior on the basis of the situation *surrounding* units – avoiding both overall structural attributes and internal unit attributes. At this level we see *international politics from a bottom-up perspective, but without falling prey to reductionism*. Situational /environment conditions are the ones that are emphasized as the interesting ones in this type of explanation. But to produce a full-fledged explanation, technically speaking, one must presuppose a specific explanatory mechanism (unit rationality, emulation, or whatever), unitary actor properties, a set of unit values, and knowledge of the resources that the unit can mobilize vis á vis the environment challenge. As mentioned in chapter 2 game theory with the proper assumptions can explain, how interaction between two units of this type may result in outcomes that were unintended by both (an arms race, for instance). One does not need overall structural explanation for that.

The type of explanation at stake here does in no way exclude that units with the same resource base react differently to the same challenges. Even if no sub-group competition (cf. chapters 6 and 7) is conceived at this level, units may react differently because they are committed to different value sets. Typically, they have different regime identities. The national actors in this book are conceptualized as *regimes*. A regime is defined here as an actor that is publicly committed to safeguarding each of the following values: its own autonomy, its identity and its control over a certain territory, including the population and material assets in this territory (Mouritzen, 1988, pp. 41-48).[1] Autonomy (or 'defensive power') is defined as the ability to avoid other actors' influence.[2] The identity category is composed of a set of specific identity values, varying from one regime to another (e.g. the values of Islamic fundamentalism, Western democracy, or apartheid). In virtue of the identity values, a regime is a less abstract unit than the state; on the other hand, it is more time persistent than the particular government in office. Regime 'subunits' are simply understood as units within the regime's control or jurisdiction that have not actively laid a distance to the regime (be it publicly or through secret collaboration with counterregimes/external powers). In other words, politically apathetic groups or individuals are seen as regime subunits in virtue of *tacit consent*. Autonomy is conceived as the basic regime value that will always be priority no.1 (cf. further pp. 116-8). There will be varying opportunities

---

1   It is typically also committed to the safeguarding of its offensive power (ability to influence others), but that is not so by definition.

2   For a survey of literature on the concepts of offensive and defensive power, cf. ibid. Some authors see 'autonomy' as covering *both* the defensive and offensive aspects of power (both 'freedom from' and 'freedom to', if they make this distinction at all); as should appear, 'autonomy' is here restricted to 'freedom from'.

for cultivating other values, including identity values. This latter category solves the problem within a state-as-actor framework of reconciling altruism with an assumptions of rational egoism. Since the regime is publicly committed to safeguarding its identity values, apparently 'altruist' policies like exporting democratic habits as part of foreign aid can be subsumed under the promotion of its identity abroad (e.g. democracy, egalitarianism). The formation of great power 'concerts' (as in post-Napoleonic Europe) is better understood in a regime perspective than a state perspective: the European royal regimes had simply their respective counter-regimes as common enemies.

For national regimes with solid legitimacy and no organized counter-regimes, the difference between 'state' and 'regime' is unimportant. Except for chapter 6 where the difference is crucially important, I shall continue to use a shifting vocabulary ('state', 'unit', 'national actor' instead of 'regime'); 'regime' may sound awkward to some readers and perhaps be confused with the popular concept of 'international regimes'.

Salient Environment and Polarity

Let us now turn to the substance of the salient environment level for the explanation of foreign policy. According to the Sprouts (1956), the 'actual' environment can be defined as '...the total aggregate of factors in space and time, to which an individual's [a unit's] behavior may be oriented or otherwise related (excepting only the environed individual's [unit's] own hereditary structures and characteristics)'(p. 12). It should be added, however, that *a certain segment of this broad setting is likely to be more relevant for the environed unit – nation-state – than the rest of it, as power and incentives wane with distance* (already introduced as 'salient environment')[3]. As pointed out by Harf et.al. (1974, p. 236), there has been a marked lack of conceptual categories exogeneous to the nation comparable to the clusters of internal variables (e.g. decision-making, bureaucracy, political parties, public opininon, interest groups) – except for systemic vocabulary, that is. Probably for this reason, the 'environment' is sometimes regarded as the homeground of specific

---

3   The definition of 'environment' by Papadakis & Starr (1987) is not very helpful, as it is virtually all-encompassing: it includes international system, international relations, societal, governmental, role and individual 'levels of environment' (p. 417). There is no particular emphasis on the external environment or, even less, any salient environment that one might expect from an 'environmental model'.

geographical peculiarities that will tend to inhibit a nomothetic orientation aiming at theory-building. This is a wrong impression. I shall provide some conceptualizations here suited to the salient environment level that should indicate its hospitality to theory-building. One might easily start with some environment features being easy to count, such as the environed unit's number of neighbours/ borders or number of IGO memberships; this would pave the way for an inductive orientation as in much quantitative conflict research (cf. the survey by Most and Starr 1989). I find it better to base theorizing on the features being of the greatest apriori *importance* to the environed unit, i.e. the naked power configurations. That brings us to the *environment polarity* as briefly presented above. This 'bottom up' conception of polarity recognizes that international politics is characterized by spatial fixity (units' non-mobility); also great powers' ability to exert power wanes with distance from their home base, ceteris paribus (Spykman 1942 p. 448; Boulding 1962, ch.12; O'Sullivan 1986, ch. 5). In the formulation of Boulding (1962 p. 231), 'the further from home any nation has to operate, the longer will be its lines of communication, and the less strength it can put in the field'. In fig. 4.1 this idea of 'loss-of-strength gradients' (the lines' slope) has been used to illustrate the situation of non-pole actors, our primary concern here. Environment polarity is simply

Fig. 4.1 Power wanes with distance from home (A,B)

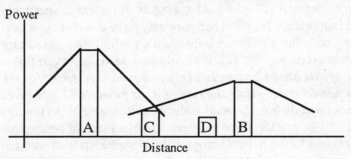

A, B: Pole actors
C: Non-pole actor, symmetric location in bipolarity
D: Non-pole actor, asymmetric location in bipolarity

the number of poles with paramount positive/negative sanctions in the neighbourhood of the environed unit. It is labelled 'unipolar', 'bipolar', 'tripolar' etc., just like systemic polarity. In fig. 4.1, the weak power in the middle (C) is surrounded by two pole powers with roughly equal abilities to project power in its area; its environment polarity is therefore 'bipolar'. In fig. 4.2 are illustrated various environment polarities[4]. A further step brings us to the *relationship between the environment poles* (if more than one), typically the trend in the balance of power between them or their mutual level of conflict (cf. chapter 5).

Fig. 4.2 Systemic vs. environment polarities in an international system

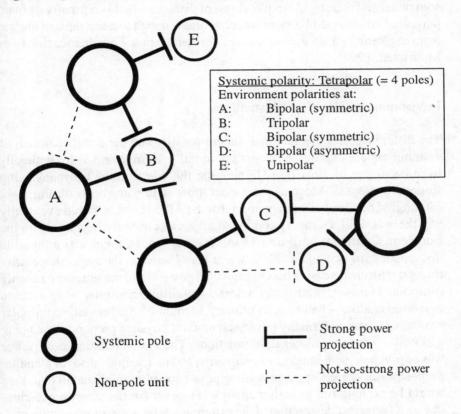

Systemic polarity: Tetrapolar (= 4 poles)
Environment polarities at:
A: Bipolar (symmetric)
B: Tripolar
C: Bipolar (symmetric)
D: Bipolar (asymmetric)
E: Unipolar

○ Systemic pole

○ Non-pole unit

⊢— Strong power projection

⌐---- Not-so-strong power projection

So much for the basic nature of the unit's salient environment; another question is how the environed unit *relates* to it. It may itself be part of this polarity by being one of its poles. One can then study its behaviour as part of one or more interactive dyads. By contrast, if the unit is a non-pole, we should

---

4   The practical problems in the counting of environment poles are not bigger (or smaller) than the counting of systemic poles (Waltz 1979 p.131), as will be illustrated in the subsequent section. The poles' power projection abilities to the area at stake are crucial instead of their 'home strengths'.

address the *constellation* that it is involved in: its location in this polarity, i.e. its basic set of relationships to the poles (in bipolarity 'symmetric', 'allied'/ 'asymmetric', cf. figs. 4.1 and 4.2)[5]. The unit may have a certain element of choice here, most clearly in the question of joining an alliance or staying outside (provided such an option is available). Depending on the credibility of an alliance, it may be able to modify the poles' power projection abilities somewhat and thereby the implications of distance – that is normally its main purpose. Dubious credibility, however, is often enough to make the unit abstain from exploiting an alliance option (cf. further chapter 7 on alliance theory or Mouritzen, 1998).

Environment Polarities: Illustrations

The difference between an environment polarity and the familiar notion of systemic polarity could be illustrated, initially, from World War II: already from december of 1941 (the US entering the war, and the Germans being stopped in front of Moscow) and even more with war events during 1942 (Stalingrad notably), it was apparent that the Allied powers would eventually win the war. Still, Germany continued to possess military hegemony on the European Continent until mid-1944. In other words, there was a tangible discrepancy for two and a half years, at least, between the systemic polarity (bipolar with an increasing bias to the Allied powers) and the European polarity (unipolar German). European actors – satellites, neutrals, or resistance movements alike – had to take primary account of the prevailing unipolar structure, because Germany possessed marked physical preponderance here and now – i.e. forceful negative sanctions. The systemic balance of power was of psychological importance, primarily, and increasingly also for planning purposes. But neglect of the prevailing power structure might entail that there would be no long run to bother about whatsoever for the actor in question, due to its physical destruction. This example – with a world war going on – should be a favourable one from the point of view of systemic explanation. And still, an actor following this systemic logic in its behaviour would seriously risk its own destruction in the meantime.

As argued in chapter 2, the importance of the salient environment explanatory level is most visible for non-pole powers; i.e. those that do not

---

5   An asymmetric location in a bipolar environment can also be labelled 'weak unipolar'; the unit is not totally dependent on the unipole.

constitute the international power structure. Whereas the international system as a whole has been characterized as bipolar during the Cold War, the polarity of relevance to Cambodia was tripolar – i.e. the US, the Soviet Union, and China being the relevant poles, possessing roughly equivalent interests and positive/negative sanctions vis à vis Cambodia.

For Sweden and Denmark in the late 1930s, the multipolar international system *as such* had very little bearing on their respective situations. Sweden's salient polarity was tripolar – Britain, Germany, and the Soviet Union being the poles. Denmark's salient polarity was bipolar between Britain and Germany, although in an asymmetric constellation: Denmark was part of Germany's 'soft sphere' of influence. Denmark found it necessary to sign a Treaty proposed by Germany in May 1939, whereas Sweden (together with Norway and Finland) could afford to decline the offer. As expressed by Chruchill in a meeting with journalists, 'unlike Denmark, they have a grave to feed the tiger over'. Hence, not only were environment polarity important at the expense of systemic polarity for both Denmark and Sweden; there were also *different* environment polarities at stake for the two countries in spite of their geographical proximity. Different policy orientations resulted.

The Gulf conflict 1990-91 was a US/ UN 'police action' against an aggressor, in case the Iraqi regime. As seen from a systemic perspective, this marked US/ UN unipolarity ('the new world order') to those, who had not yet understood its implications. However, the polarity in *Jordan's* salient environment was bipolar during the whole Gulf crisis; the US/ UN and Iraq could both project significant power and influence towards Jordan. An implication of this was that Jordan could not participate in UN sanctions against Iraq. *Even* in moments of 'new world order' triumph – as for instance the initial decision 1935 in the League of Nations on sanctions against Italy after her attack on Abyssinia – geopolitics prevailed at the local level. Italy's immediate neighbours voted no to sanctions or abstained – although they could have more reason than others to hope for the curbing of the aggressor[6].

Poland or most other Warsaw Pact countries during the Cold War could illustrate the difference between regional polarity and environment polarity. The regional European polarity that Poland was part of was bipolar (the NATO/ WAPA 'security complex'), just like the systemic polarity. However, Poland's environment polarity was Moscow unipolar. That is to say: there was *one* actor with paramount negative and positive sanctions in relation to Poland: the Soviet Union. No Western actor could rival the Soviet power and influence

---

6   Only Austria, Hungary, and Albania (apart from Italy herself) voted against sanctions.

in Warsaw. Of course, Western rearmament or increased tension between the two blocs could indirectly affect Poland, but that would in turn have to be mediated through Soviet decision (be it on rearmament, troop redeployments, repression in Poland, or whatever). There was one paramount actor to worry about and relate to in Warsaw: the Soviet Union.

European Heterogeneities 1989-94: From the Hague to Kiev

The European *regional* power structure that emerged after the end of the Cold War was EC/EU[7] unipolar; that is, the EU became the paramount power pole on the European continent. I shall show that even if this overall European picture was necessary for understanding the situations of individual nation-states, it was far from sufficient. There were wide-ranging heterogeneities as to salient environments across the continent.

Let me first, however, describe the overall European power structure. The paramount power pole has few purely negative sanctions (trade embargo, e.g.) and no military means of its own. Through the gradual downfall of the Eastern pole from 1988, definitely completed with the disintegration of the Soviet Union in 1991, this absence of military means was no longer an impediment to EU pole status. Its most crucial sanctions are its trade barriers to the world around or, in positive terms, varying degrees of access to its market – the world's largest 'internal market'. Its pole position is also based on political prestige – being the 'good company'. This, in turn, is based on two things: being rich, at least relatively speaking, and being 'Europe'. The EU has managed to acquire almost monopoly on this positively value-loaded term.

What distinguishes the EU pole, however, from all poles in modern history, is the fact that it is a supra-national international entity with nation-states as members – in other words a hitherto unknown entity that one could label a 'membership pole'. Moreover, it wishes further members, and nation-states outside the pole do actually wish to become such. Hence, the pole is gradually expanding. This seems, so far, to be a self-reinforcing process: the bigger the pole, the larger its market, and the more desirable it becomes to get inside for those still outside; moreover, growth implies that the monopoly on the 'Europe' label becomes increasingly justified.

---

7   The EC became the EU on 1 November 1993, as the EU Treaty had been ratified in all member-countries. I shall consistently say the 'EU' below, even though events both before and after this date are discussed.

Still, the EU has a somewhat ephemeral pole identity. Whereas the EU may be the core of Europe, there is no 'core of the core' (Buzan et al. 1990, p. 218). This means that the pole has low self-control (Mouritzen 1997b pp. 96-101); it is easy for outsiders to penetrate and play off various subunits (nation-states, primarily, but also the Commission) against each other. Also, the pole's decision procedure (unanimity) in 'foreign policy' issues favours, evidently, lowest common denominator decisions and entails sometimes paralysis.

This does not really detract from the EU pole character, as its positive sanctions and prestige seem to remain largely unaffected all over Europe. The number of accommodators seems to be increasing rather than decreasing – as does their willingness to accommodate. But it constitutes an essential difference compared to virtually all previously existing poles.

Let us turn to the situations of individual nation-states. Mouritzen, Wæver & Wiberg (1996) analysed the challenges facing a range of European nation-states in the semi-decade following the fall of the Berlin Wall. Particular focus was aimed at the following six: two EU insiders (Denmark and the Netherlands), two would-be insiders (Finland and Poland), and two outsiders (Lithuania and the Ukraine). Comparing the challenges facing the six demonstrated the heterogeneity of their salient environments (Mouritzen 1996a). The events/regions as sources of major challenges facing the six nation-states have been crudely summarized in figure 4.3.

Only one of the challenges was actually common to all six: developments in EU integration. In virtue of the prevailing European unipolarity, such developments affected all six – albeit differently in different constellations. German unification, by contrast, was a process of *vital* importance to Germany's neighbours, only – i.e. Poland, Denmark, and the Netherlands among those analyzed here (in that order of significance). The Soviet disintegration was,

Fig. 4.3 Events/regions as sources of major challenges

	Den.	Neth.	Fin.	Pol.	Lit.	Ukr.
German unification	•	•		•		
EC/EU integration	•	•	•	•	•	•
Central European cooperation				•	•	•
Soviet disintegration and Russia			•	•		•
NATO	•			•	•	(•)
"New World Order"	•	•	•			
Second and Third World	•	•	•			
Norden, Baltic region	•		•		•	

evidently, a major event for the overall systemic polarity, in the sense that the prospects for a re-emerging bipolarity disappeared. But it was only in Finland, Poland, Lithuania and the Ukraine that the Soviet disintegration came to mark a watershed: the two former because they were neighbours to the Soviet Union, and the two latter because they were part of it and, hence, gained their status as nation-states of their own. The selected cases can be ordered on a stability spectrum from West to East, in rough outline: the Netherlands representing ultra-stability (apart from a little nervous twitch upon the German unification), Denmark experiencing shifts in her EU integration enthusiasm (the EU supposedly binding Germany), Finland shifting her basic foreign policy orientation (cf. chapters 5, 7), Poland witnessing the birth of a new (democratic) regime and Lithuania and the Ukraine being (re)born as nation-states in the first place. The 'Soviet connection' – or its absence – was the *key* to understanding this stability spectrum, whereas the 'German connection' was the efficient cause behind the relatively minor Dutch and Danish disturbances.

One thing is that *systemic* polarity usually deviates significantly from environment polarity; the observation here is that even *regional* (European) unipolarity deviates from environment polarities – which also deviate among each other. There was not 'one Europe' challenging all European states in the same way. With Russian reassertion during 1993 and 1994, trying to include the CIS in its 'soft sphere', the Kiev environment polarity tended to shift from being a EU unipolar based one to possibly a bipolar one with Brussels and Moscow as the poles (Poulsen-Hansen & Wæver 1996 pp. 231-2). The fact that the Netherlands or Denmark were so relatively unaffected by the Soviet disintegration or later the 'Zhirinovsky effect', whereas the other four were vitally affected, may sound trivial to any sane journalist or political analyst. But the virtual neglect of this locational factor (and thereby the national 'frog perspective' on polarity) in major IR theorizing as demonstrated in chapter 3 necessitates the stressing of observations of this kind.

Along with environment polarity, the notion of constellation defined above is a means to bridge the gap between regional polarity and (divergent) national environments. It rejects the tacit assumption that all national units face one and the same polarity. But conversely, it does not fall prey to the temptation of saying that all units' situations/ salient environments are unique. They are classified into broad categories that provide a link to regional polarity. Regarding a unipolar membership pole in a process of integration – as the EU from 1989 – the constellations are those of 'insiders', 'would-be insiders', and 'outsiders'. These categories should be rather straightforward to define in an EU context. The 'insiders' are the EU members, simply. The 'would-be insiders' are potential members in the sense that they see membership as desirable and realistic, be it in the near or mid-term future (a decade). The 'outsiders' are those that either do not *want* membership in the first place, or realize that their possibilities of obtaining it are negligible, anyway, within the nearest decade or so. Also, they should be stipulated as being more dependent on our pole in question than upon any other corresponding pole in the international system – but not necessarily located in geographic Europe. In geographical terms, there is reason to believe in a kind of center-periphery relationship between the constellations: the insiders are likely to form a kind of European core, the would-be insiders comprise a second layer, whereas the outsiders constitute an outer fringe (cf. fig. 4.4). As a quick glance at a map will reveal, however, exceptions can be found.

Fig. 4.4 Three constellations in unipolar Europe 1989-94

A few crucial specifications should be added to the constellation typology in an EU context. Firstly, the essence of the typology is a belief that the constellations actually correspond to three separate and easily discernible 'steps' in reality. But secondly, we allow for certain minor formal heterogeneites regarding the insiders (e.g. the Danish or British 'special arrangements' connected to the Maastricht Treaty) and the would-be insiders (i.e. more or less intimate types of affiliation with the EU). That is to say: the steps are not altogether even or well-polished (Wiberg 1996). Thirdly, though, the heterogeneities (present or future) are/will be of a cumulative nature. In other words: the steps are/will be consistently sloping. As argued by Wæver (1993, pp. 36, 38), a 'Europe à la carte', where each can pick and choose its favourite menu, is unlikely. There has to be a centre, a core that runs the process as a comprehensive package deal, encompassing at least the two essential powers (Germany and France); otherwise 'Europe' would lose its most basic actor properties (cf. also Maclay 1992, pp. 4, 26; Michalski & Wallace 1992)[8].

Prior to 1989 the distinction between systemic and regional polarity, notably, was partly invisible: as Europe was overlayed (Buzan, 1991) by systemic bipolarity (Europe being the central arena of confrontation between the superpowers) and as the superpowers – or NATO and WAPA – were each others' salient environments, the distinction did not matter much for practical purposes. The constellations – symmetrics, allies/ asymmetrics – made a difference, of course. In the post-Cold War era, however, Europe acquired a marked regional power structure of its own. Whereas it was of little more than academic interest for European non-pole actors to know whether the international system, as seen from a bird's eye view, was US unipolar, tripolar, or even multipolar, it was more important that the regional polarity was EU unipolar. And it was even more significant whether they were EU unipole insiders, would-be insiders, or outsiders. Moreover, there were further factors pushing in a 'non-systemic' and even 'non-regional' direction. The proliferation of new states in East – and Central Europe and in the ex-Soviet Union meant a corresponding proliferation of new borders – most of them disputed, actually – and thereby also a proliferation of new and mutually diverging salient environments (as an arithmetic fact). The many disputed borders led to further local polarities, such as the Balkan system of polarities. The EU polarity was the most basic one for understanding the salient environments of the whole Continent, whereas the new emerging polarities were relevant, mainly, to the specific geographical areas at stake. That means that they affected some would-be insiders and, even more, virtually all of the outsiders. The EU polarity was necessary, but far from sufficient for understanding salient environments and thereby basic policy preconditions throughout the continent.

---

8   The *theoretical* fruitfulness of this constellation typology will be evaluated in chapter 7.

5 Testing Theories

With the fragmented picture of international politics presented in the pre-theory so far, it is not possible or desirable to present one overarching (global) theory of international politics. Several theoretical constructs are compatible with the pre-theory of international politics that has been argued in chapters 2, 3, and 4. In this chapter, three specific theoretical constructs will be formulated and tested. They all explain aspects of foreign policy (the dependent variable) from features of the national unit's salient environment. The independent variable is tension between the strong powers in the first theory and balance of power between them in the second one. In both theories, the constellation (symmetric vs. asymmetric) that the national unit is involved in functions as parameter for the propositions. That is to say: the foreign policy effects of tension shifts or balance of power shifts are widely different or even inverse, depending on constellation.

Whereas general aspects of foreign policy are at stake in the first and second theories (its strategies/level of activity vs. its balancing/bandwagoning between the power poles), the third construct – a simple geopolitical model – seeks to explain a foreign policy engagement in a specific geographical area.

Tension between the Strong and the Strategy of the Weak[1]

I shall first present and test a constellation theory consisting of two sets of specific propositions. It is asserted that exposing identical units to identical stimuli will lead to inverse behavioural reactions because of different natures of their salient environments. The latter will be held as parameter in each set:

For a (non-pole) nation-state involved in a *symmetric* constellation in a bipolar environment (cf. fig. 4.2),
(1a) the higher the level of tension between the two poles, the higher its offensive power,
(1b) the higher the level of tension between the two poles, the lower its defensive power, and
(1c) the higher the level of tension between the two poles, the more *activated*

---

1   Instead of 'pole powers' vs. 'non-pole power' I shall sometimes talk about the 'strong' and the 'weak' in this chapter, for the sake of linguistic variation. As will be argued, however, the concept of 'small state' is avoided.

its behaviour, applying the strategies of non-commitment, counterweight and, possibly, mediation.

For a (non-pole) nation-state involved in an *asymmetric* constellation in a bipolar environment (cf. fig. 4.2),

(2a) as the level of tension between the two poles increases, its offensive power will remain roughly unaffected,

(2b) as the level of tension between the two poles increases, its defensive power will be affected both favorably and disfavorably simultaneously, and

(2c) as the level of tension between the two poles increases, its behaviour will be de-activated.

The theoretical justification regarding the symmetric constellation runs as follows: offensive power (= ability to exert influence) increases, because the 'market value' of the nation's (below: unit's) assets increases with rising pole tension (Goldmann, 1979); the unit can exploit tension between the poles (1a)[2]. The reverse side of the coin, however (1b), is that the unit is also more *exposed* during high tension (Rothstein, 1968, p. 192); its defensive power wanes (= autonomy, i.e. ability to resist the offensive power of other units). The risk of pre-emption increases: the higher value ascribed to the unit's assets, the easier the poles will be tempted to gain control over them, in the expectation that the assets might otherwise fall under the control of the conflicting pole. In order to forestall the danger of pre-emption, the unit must increasingly signal its non-committed course between the poles (strategy of non-commitment, 'neutrality'). The newly improved offensive power also paves the way for a more assertive posture. Non-commitment will be more credible, if supported by a certain level of military strength and preparedness (strategy of counterweight); this will reduce the risk of (successful) pre-emption. A strategy of détente and mediation may be used in order to reduce the dangerous pole tension. The improved offensive power makes this realistic, and such a strategy will also bolster the unit's prestige and thereby both offensive and defensive power. In sum, the increased stressing of non-commitment, the emphasis on military counterweight and the incentive to mediate between the poles all amount to an *activation* of behaviour (1c).

Presupposing instead an asymmetrical constellation, no increase in offensive power can be expected (2a). The unit cannot exploit the increasing pole conflict, since it is obviously part of one pole's 'soft sphere' (Vloyantes, 1975, pp. 22-28) – its paramount pole. To try to switch dependencies would

---

2   Tension is understood here straightforwardly as the (degree of) expectation of conflict behaviour between actors (Goldmann 1979, p. 117).

be far too dangerous to be credible as seen from any of the poles. The market value of its assets remains unaffected, hence. For the same reason, pre-emption will be unlikely (2b); it is unnecessary from the viewpoint of the paramount power, whereas it will be seen as a reckless enterprise from the conflicting pole. Additionally, our unit will enjoy a scarcity advantage as tension increases. There will be a scarcity of attention, as the poles focus on their major conflict; also, they will make up a tighter priority list of what is really relevant for it. The poles' pursuit of 'luxury values' that may bother our unit during low tension (e.g. ideology promotion, territorial appetites with no strategic relevance for the major conflict) will disappear during high tension. On the other hand, demands *actually* forthcoming from the paramount power to our unit will be more specific and less negotiable now; the paramount power knows better than before, what it really wants (its tighter priority list). Whether these demands can outweigh the absence of luxury pressure can hardly be derived theoretically; it is impossible to say, whether aggregate defensive power will improve or be reduced.

During low tension, our unit has anticipated the wishes of the paramount power and reconciled them with what was cheapest according to its own value system ('demand anticipation'). During high tension, however, it would be foolish to anticipate too much (2c). That might result in redundant concessions, as the 'necessary' ones would have to be given anyway, according to the paramount power's tightened priority list. Moreover, if the unit benefits from a scarcity of attention, there is no reason to spoil this by drawing attention to itself. On the other hand, when the 'necessary' demands are actually raised, their low negotiability will lead to quick decisions to comply. In sum, these arguments amount to a low key posture; the asymmetrically located unit will *de-activate* its behaviour with rising tension: no demand anticipation or other attention-drawing behaviour.

Sweden on the Stage and Finland on the Balcony. These two sets of propositions will now be tested on Swedish and Finnish reactions to the increasing superpower tension in the early 1980s (the 'New Cold War')[3]. The balance of power between the superpower poles – a potentially disturbing factor for such a test – can be seen as roughly constant during the period at stake. Sweden

---

3   The intermediary reasoning behind the behavioural propositions 1c and 2c is not commented upon, unless the expectations turn out to be wrong. Obviously, correspondence between expectations and observations does not prove the underlying assumptions to be valid. But discussion of them is seen as more urgent when our expectations do not fit with observations.

was involved in environment bipolarity and placed roughly symmetrically between two power poles: the Soviet Union and the US (NATO). Sweden was about equally crucial to military planning in the two blocs. Finland, by contrast, fulfills the criterion of an asymmetrical constellation: since September 1944, her belonging to the Soviet 'soft sphere' had been more or less explicitly recognized by the poles (Vloyantes, 1975). The NATO military power posture had repercussions on Finland, but NATO did not attempt to rival the Soviet Union on Finnish territory in case of military conflict.

Rising pole *tension,* the independent variable in all propositions, was the identical stimulus that both Sweden and Finland were exposed to. Tension between the superpowers rose significantly towards the end of the 1970s, but the truly dramatic increase came with the Soviet invasion of Afghanistan at the end of December 1979 and NATO'S INF decision on 12 December. Most of the European NATO members tried desperately to rescue as much of the European detente as possible; indeed, they succeeded to a certain extent, despite events in Poland 1980-81. The Nordic area, characterized by relatively low strategic interest in the postwar era, had been ascribed a greater military significance even prior to these events. As regards Sweden, various Soviet (and other?) submarine intrusions in her territorial waters (the archipelago) became politicized from 1981, when they gained public attention. It can, of course, always be discussed whether or not such intrusions should be interpreted independently from the superpower relationship. Tunander has argued convincingly (1989, pp. 108-120) that the intrusions should be seen as a Soviet response to the US forward maritime strategy in Northern waters and to the NATO INF decision, pedagogically illustrating to Sweden and others the impossibility of keeping Swedish territory nuclear-free by military means. The sometimes rather overt intrusions, supplemented by various Soviet semi-official hints, should encourage a more 'active' Swedish policy of neutrality, approaching the Finnish model. Such a policy might promote Nordic or European nuclear-free zones politically (in contrast to anti-submarine combat) or strive for a ban on cruise missiles. NATO cruise missiles fired towards Soviet territory from the Norwegian Sea could hardly avoid violating Sweden's air space and, hence, her neutrality[4].

The *Swedish response* to this development seems to conform neatly to the expectations in proposition 1c. Firstly, the strategy of military counterweight was somewhat strengthened. The proposed cuts in the military budget for

---

4   The interpretation of the submarine intrusions by Leitenberg (1987) stresses somewhat more the conceiveable Soviet military motives, but in no way rules out Tunander's interpretation.

1982-87 were greatly reduced (though not eliminated; Bjøl 1986, pp. 38-39). The means for antisubmarine combat were significantly improved. Radar equipment to combat cruise missiles was produced and a new generation of Swedish-built figther-planes was decided upon in 1982. In March 1982, the Swedish army held its largest manoeuvre since World War II (against an 'attack from the East'). All these decisions and the publicity surrounding them amount to an increased emphasis on the strategy of military counterweight.

Secondly, a range of initiatives seems to indicate a strengthening of the strategy of detente and mediation. One such initiative was the decision to host the conference on confidence-building measures, the Stockholm conference 1984-86, which was decided upon in 1983. The proposal of the Palme Commision, headed by the then Swedish prime minster, regarding a nuclear-free zone in Central Europe was advocated on behalf of the Swedish government without the qualifications regarding the level of conventional military balance in Europe, originally made by the Commision (Palme, 1982). In 1983, Sweden voted in the UN together with Finland for an East proposal regarding no first use of nuclear weapons.

It can, of course, be disputed whether these decisions represented the strategy of detente and mediation only, or whether they also expressed a more narrow wish to strengthen Sweden's own neutrality image (the strategy of non-commitment). In view of the Western nature of Swedish society, the main credibility problem with Swedish non-commitment has always been eastwards. Additionally, a somewhat Western-biased image had been created during the non-socialist government (which resigned in 1982) due to a few 'undiplomatic' incidents (Bjøl, 1986, pp. 39-40). So it seems that the Palme government, through these decisions, was trying to tighten up Sweden's neutrality image. A large-scale military manoeuvre in mid-Sweden during the winter of 1985 against 'an attack from the West' was presumably meant to neutralize the 1982 manoeuvre. The visit to the United States by the Conservative parliamentarian Carl Bildt in April 1983 was criticized by the government (Jervas, 1987, p. 72).

Thus, we observe an *activation* of Swedish policy in the early 1980s through increased emphasis on the strategies of counterweight, detente and mediation and non-commitment. There were no significant tendencies towards 'rocking the boat': borrowing counterweight from NATO through some kind of treaty arrangement (occasionally suggested in the press) or an adaptive acquiescence posture (Mouritzen 1988) approaching the Finnish one. As to the latter: even though one might interpret the UN voting mentioned above as a slight accommodation to Soviet preferences, the publication of the 'Submarine

Report' in 1983 (SOU, 1983) and the accompanying official protest to the Soviet Union (Tunander, 1989, pp. 117-120) were rather steps of defiance. We can conclude for the moment, hence, that the expectations described in *1c* have been fulfilled as far as the present case is concerned.

According to the then Finnish-Soviet Friendship and Cooperation Treaty, *Finland* and the Soviet Union were to consult on common military measures if threats to either country's security appeared from Germany or powers allied with Germany (NATO) over Finnish territory. Such consultations would, of course, shatter the fragile neutrality status that Finland had established since the mid-1950s. Thus it was an essential aim of Finnish policy to avoid consultations. Since the early 1960s one means towards this aim was an 'active peace policy' to reduce Soviet fears or pretexts for pressure on Finland (consultations). Crucial in this active peace policy had been the recurrent proposals for ratification of a Nordic nuclear weapon-free zone. In view of the framework described here, the peace policy both anticipated Soviet preferences ('demand anticipation') and also served Finland's own interest (running parallel in this question)[5].

The Finnish position was much improved through the German-Soviet detente that was partially retained during the escalation of superpower tension. Undeniably, potential dangers existed: a Soviet wish for consultations could be provoked by NATO cruise missiles that might violate Finnish air space on their way to the Soviet Union, or by the 1981 agreement to pre-position heavy equipment for the US Marine Corps in Norway (a reaction to the expansion of the Soviet Murmansk fleet).

On the basis of proposition 2c, we should expect a reduction in Finnish 'demand anticipation' in the new and tense situation. This means less anticipation of presumed Soviet preferences, such as peace offensives in the region. We should, in other words, expect a de-activation of the Finnish posture (cf. also Hakovirta, 1982, p. 50) that might resemble the 'lie low' posture of President Paasikivi during the classic Cold War. Something in this direction seems actually to have happened. President Koivisto, who came into office at about the time of rapid tension escalation (1981), adopted a far more discreet, low-key posture than President Kekkonen (Väyrynen, 1983, p. 163; Väyrynen, 1987, pp. 43,52,54). Gone were the frequent peace initiatives of the Kekkonen era, culminating in Finland's hosting the CSCE conference in 1975. Appeals

---

5   Hakovirta (1982, p. 41-42) argues along these lines that Finland was a country with an exceptionally strong national interest in tension reduction. This argument, however, presupposes that there was no risk of 'luxury pressure' from the Soviet Union in times of detente.

for a treaty on a Nordic nuclear weapon-free zone became less frequent.

The only significant exceptions to this low-key posture were various presidential statements in favour of a ban on cruise missiles, in line with Kekkonen's frequently expressed attitude[6]. This deviation from expectations can, however, be reasonably explained. Finland, by virtue of its existing and highly explicit treaty with the Soviet Union, faced one of the most predictable, though not very likely, threat scenarios imaginable. Hence, striving for a ban on cruise missiles would never be a 'redundant concession'. Given the text of the treaty and the stable behavioural pattern surrounding it from both sides, the interests of both countries were quite obvious as regards, for instance, cruise missiles. Thus, Finland's statements on this issue are hardly surprising[7].

In sum, while subject to the same systemic influence (tension) and both being 'small powers' with similar domestic political systems (and similar archipelagos hospitable to submarine intrusion), Sweden and Finland were affected not only differently but actually *inversely:* Sweden's policy was activated and Finland's de-activated. Sweden found itself on the stage of Great Power rivalry, whereas Finland took its place 'in the balcony' (an expression used by President Kolvisto, 1983; cf. Väyrynen, 1987, pp. 47, 49). Not even the cooling down of Swedish-Soviet relations with the politicization of submarine intrusions affected neighbouring Finland adversely.

Expectations derived from the constellation theory have, by and large, held water in the cases at hand. The minor deviation found in the Finnish case could be reasonably well accounted for. One could object, of course, that the fulfilment of expectations was due to exogenous factors rather than to the virtues of the constellation theory. Such objections are tempting in the face of a relatively simple theoretical construct with only one dynamic explanatory factor (tension). For instance, the military-strategic factor rather than international tension might account for much (e.g. Jervas, 1987, p. 57). As seen here, however, the two factors are closely intertwined, as illustrated by the double-track decision and the subsequent deployment – and dismantling – of the US INF missiles (cf. also Andren, 1982, p. 63; Tunander, 1989, p. 116). It might also be objected that the increased Swedish emphasis on the counterweight strategy was more due to domestic political considerations

---

6   For instance Koivisto's speech on nuclear weapons in March 1983 to the Finnish Parliament and in October the same year to the UN General Assembly (Väyrynen, 1987, p. 43); also his New Year speech 1985.

7   As to 'demands emanating from the paramount power', no manifest demands were actually made during the period considered here; thus, the question of reactions to such demands is irrelevant in this context.

than a reaction to external events (Agrell, 1983). But even if this were true, the soil would still have to be fertile: in other words, public opinion would have had to be affected by the tense international and regional climate (Agrell, 1983, pp. 367-368).

Balancing vs. Bandwagoning: Testing Balance-of-Power Theory

Also the second specific theory to be formulated and tested is rooted in states' salient environment; instead of tension between the strong powers the independent variable is this time the balance of power between them. As with the previous theory, the state's constellation functions as parameter.

The failed Soviet coup of 19-21 August 1991 and the ensuing dissolution of the Soviet Union and its ideology provides excellent opportunities to investigate, to what extent shifts in the balance of power in weak states' salient environments can account for their policy changes. Typically, theories stressing the balance of power factor are at a disadvantage compared to most other theories seeking to explain foreign policy, because visible changes in their core explanatory factor happen infrequently, so that the factor is easily forgotten or, at best, taken for granted. The best opportunities to challenge balance of power theories occur in connection with wide-ranging *and* sudden power shifts. The short time span implies that other explanatory factors have fewer chances to blur the impact of the balance of power factor. This means typically dramatic 'turning points' in world history such as major wars or the collapse of empires in the wake of revolutions. As an example could be mentioned studies of the 'turn of the tide' during World War II and how it affected the position of a number of weak powers and their foreign policy strategies (e.g. Baker Fox 1959, Mouritzen 1988 chs. 10-12). The shift in the Central European balance of power in late 1989 and the beginning of 1990 (the East European revolutions and the German unification) also seems sufficiently wide-ranging and sudden to provide promising analytic opportunities.

I think that even better opportunities are presented by the situation analysed in this section. For a number of weak powers, the balance of power in their salient environments changed dramatically and suddenly. The communist coup implied that the Soviet Union seemed to be re-emerging as a *military* superpower during those couple of days that its success seemed likely. Ideological bipolarity was re-established, and the Western reactions strongly condemning the coup could lead one to expect a future conflictual East-West relationship in general terms. In other words, the amorphous and sleeping bipolarity that had existed under Gorbachev prior to the coup seemed to become real bipolarity. As the failure of the coup became evident on its third day (Wednesday, 21 August), not only did this polarity melt away as quickly as it had emerged; status quo prior to the coup did *not* get a chance to re-establish itself. The communist party was suspended in the Russian republic, and soon the rest of the republics followed track. Even though President Gorbachev was restored, his power base was rapidly undermined, as declarations of independence were issued by the various Soviet republics, one after the other during the week that followed. The independences of the Baltic republics won wide international recognition within a couple of weeks after the coup. The conservative forces within the KGB and the army who had initiated the coup seemed to be eliminated, thus significantly reducing the risk of another attempted take-over. Within one or two weeks, hence, bipolarity manifestly re-emerged, was dissolved again, and then the actor being one of the potential power poles seemed to disappear, paving the way for EU unipolarity across the whole continent (cf. chapter 4). It is an understatement to say that this was a wideranging shift in the balance of power, given the fact that post-war bipolarity actually *disappeared.* Moreover, this happened during an even shorter time-span than the 1989-90 events mentioned above. So the opportunities to challenge a theory on 'the balance of power between the strong and the policies of the weak' seem to be favourable, indeed[8].

Bandwagoning: A Trend Conceptualization

Baker Fox (1959) found in her study of small states during World War II that 'anti-balance of power behaviour' (bandwagoning) was typical for them, and she suggested that such behaviour might characterize small-states generally (ibid. p. 187)[9]. Instead of trying to restore the balance of power like the classical 'holder of the balance' (e.g. Britain) would do, the small state's support is rendered to the probable winner. Through this form of bandwagoning, or

---

8   The level of tension (conflict) between the two poles varied dramatically even during the short time-span, we are considering here. Hence, the balance of power factor was not alone on the stage. However, as I have shown in the preceding section, the tension factor affects the weak powers' *level* of activity rather than the substance of their policies that we shall consider here. Therefore it does not really blur the picture, as one could have feared.

9   She hints a certain doubt, though, regarding the applicability of this hypothesis to post-World War II small states (ibid.)

'weathercock policy' as critics would say, a contribution – however modest – is made towards an even more askew balance of power. Top priority is given to safeguarding the small state's core values in the short run; otherwise, there may be no long run to bother about. It cannot afford the luxury of trying to safeguard its long-term interest in a more balanced polarity (ibid. p. 181; cf. also Rothstein (1968) pp. 11-12; Handel (1981) p. 29). Mouritzen (1988) found that Danish foreign policy in the 1930s and Swedish and Danish policy during World War II bandwagoned in neat correspondence with the balance of power in their salient environments (chs. 10-12). As expressed by Rothstein (1968):

> Small Powers threatened by neighboring Great Powers... in the course of Great Power conflicts, were forced to play a perilous game: moving quickly from the lighter to the heavier side of the balance as soon as an apparent victor in any contest could be discerned. (p. 11).

He adds, normatively, 'if power corrupts, so does the lack of it'. Not specifically concerned with small states, there has been a debate on bandwagoning vs. balancing in alliance politics (Waltz 1979, Walt 1987, Labs 1992, Kaufman 1992, Walt 1992).

Behind the disagreements on what is the typical form of behaviour can often be found different definitions of the central concepts at stake. Some specifications and comments to the bandwagoning (anti-balance of power) hypothesis should be made here. There are no aspirations to observe or measure any absolute balance whatsoever. Even if this might be meaningful, it would present considerable practical problems. What is possible, however, is the observation of clear-cut trends in this balance, including major turning-points. Correspondingly, it is possible to analyse *trends,* including major shifts, in (weak power) policies. In other words, the concept of bandwagoning is meaningful diachronically. 'Supporting the winner' refers, hence, to the trend-winner – who may be the under-dog in absolute terms. And 'support' may actually mean a less hostile attitude than previously.

With this trend-stipulation of 'bandwagoning', I seem to differ from the literature that was referred to above (although certain formulations implicitly reveal a trend focus). A status instead of a trend focus prevails (e.g. Labs 1992 note 2). As formulated by Walt (1992):

> Properly understood, bandwagoning means aligning with the strongest or most threatening state, thereby rendering it more powerful but also more benign (or so the bandwagoning state hopes) (p. 471).

By this definition, other ways of rendering the powerful more powerful and benign – such as making one's neutrality more 'friendly' – are excluded from sight. Through Walt's narrow definitions of both bandwagoning and balancing, several in-between positions are neglected. As pointed out by Kaufman (1992 p. 437), referring to postures vis à vis the Nazi threat, neither the British policy of appeasement, nor French indecision, nor American aloofness, nor Polish neutrality, falls strictly into either category. By contrast, a trend distinction between bandwagoning and balancing is logically exhaustive (either one moves one way or the other or not at all). A status perspective makes the distinction non-exhaustive: there will be an arbitrary number of statuses in-between, as hinted by Kaufman's examples (cf. also Labs 1992 pp. 392-4).

Parameter and Theoretical Justifications

There is one further modification, however, that should be made in relation to Baker Fox's hypothesis. Bandwagoning is not necessarily characteristic of 'small states'; the decisive parameter is that the unit in question is subject to unipolarity in its salient environment: that there is *one* power pole here that is paramount on positive/negative sanctions in relation to the unit in question. That applies to *unipolarity* with no conflicting pole in sight (cf. fig.4.2), but also to a unit *asymmetrically located* between two poles (the asymmetric constellation). Bandwagoning may also occur somewhat beyond the unipole sphere, but that is less frequent.

The small state literature is rich on discussions concerning the proper definition of 'small state'[10]. The focus here on salient polarity instead of size makes it unnecessary to delve into the essence of 'smallness'. We can happily ignore the question, whether the involved states are 'really' small powers or not.

The underlying reasoning presupposed here is that during unipolarity (asymmetric bipolarity), the weak is in a geopolitically highly dependent position vis à vis one power pole. This paramount power possesses significant negative sanctions that the weak anticipates (manifest threats are usually redundant). As the balance of power tips even more in favour of the paramount power, its negative sanctions also increase, and the assets of the weak are not requested to the same extent as before. Unilateral dependency has become more pronounced[11].

---

10   For a survey and discussion, cf. Christmas-Møller 1983.

11   The trends described here are, evidently, exacerbated, if the paramount power constitutes the essential *dynamics* of the balance of power shift: if it, e.g., goes through a rapid re-armament process or, conversely, if its power base is being undermined or even disintegrated.

In order to prevent the negative sanctions from materializing, i.e. in order to retain status quo, the weak will have to sweeten status quo to the paramount power more than before. In other words, in addition to a favourable balance of power development, the paramount power is rewarded with some *extra* benefits. This is bandwagoning as stipulated above. Conversely, if the balance tips to the disfavour of the paramount power, inverse tendencies will be found. The weak power may even be able to jump into an opposing alliance or, more often, to a roughly symmetric position between two power poles (one of them being the former paramount pole). Also this is bandwagoning: the strong power is 'punished' for its weakened position, so that it may be further weakened[12].

A unipole with negative sanctions will always be dangerous in some sense to its environment, also when it reaches its low ebb; one can always make worst case scenarios for the future. The crucial question for the surrounding units therefore is not whether it is desirable to jump out of dependence; it is rather when it is *possible*. For pure power reasons, that is probably near to the low ebb of the continuum.

Let us now turn to a member of an *opposing alliance*. Such a unit, including a weak power, will not typically engage in bandwagoning. Its reason for joining the alliance in the first place was typically to borrow military or other counterweight from a strong power in the face of a perceived increasing threat (thereby reinforcing a salient bipolarity, probably). This balancing is the opposite of bandwagoning, in the sense that a contribution was offered towards balancing off the increased threat. In connection with periods of specific tension, allied powers will seek to balance again through, e.g., a re-armament effort or a specific alert. Correspondingly, should the other side become more friendly or even break down, they will lower their guard.

However, the freedom of manoeuvre is typically more significant for the weak allied than for the weak in other constellations (except, of course, for allied satellites). The range of behaviour, hence, is broader, giving more leeway for the influence of domestic factors in a rather unpredictable direction. One factor, however, that one can consider apriori in a systematic way is the seriousness of the external threat. Let us assume that it can be high, medium, or low. In the former case, the weak *has to* be extra loyal to its pole and thereby usually rather hostile to the threatening power, for fear of being abandoned by its protector. In the latter case, the weak can *afford* such a hostile attitude.

---

12   The theory will be somewhat refined in chapter 7 (I have presupposed a status quo ('conservative') unipole here). It should be added that the bandwagon argument also applies to a 'pole of attraction', a unipole with predominantly positive sanctions; cf. the self-reinforcing mechanisms in relation to EU enlargement (cf. pp. 105-6).

It is in a position to express its identity or other values that will typically be in conflict with those of the threatening actor (its reason for joining the alliance originally). With a *medium* threat, however, a more cautious attitude of non-provocation is called for. The weak has a lot to lose in this situation; there is no reason to provoke high tension in its own salient environment, thereby ultimately turning its own territory into a battlefield (entrapment)[13]. Now, what is interesting here are the trends. With 3 levels of threat, we get 6 changes and 3 constants (e.g. from low to low threat). If the reasonings above are plausible, we get 2 developments (out of 9) that will cause bandwagoning: from medium to low threat perception, or from low to medium. In the latter case, the balance of power has shifted to the advantage of the perceived enemy, and this has entailed, specifically, that the weak has become more exposed (typically a frontline state). Hence, it has lowered its profile and become more cautious in its behaviour vis à vis the threat. This is a way of 'rewarding' the trend-winner, in other words bandwagoning. Conversely from medium to low threat perception: as the balance of power has shifted in disfavour of the threat, and specifically has reduced the threat from medium to low, the weak can now abandon its former attitude of non-provocation. In other words, the perceived enemy is 'punished' for being a trend-loser. This is also bandwagoning. The rest of the transitions need not be commented upon here; they will lead to either balancing or unaffected behaviour on the part of the weak ally[14].

Turning to a third constellation, a *symmetric* one during bipolarity, the weak is in a roughly similar relationship to the two strong powers. Non-commitment in relation to both poles is the core strategy. If the balance of power tips in one or the other direction, the weak must, in order to stay roughly symmetric, move somewhat in that direction. But this is obviously bandwagoning, as the strengthened power pole will be a bit further strengthened in this way. However, this type of behaviour will be less pronounced than in the asymmetric/unipolar constellation: due to its symmetric position, the local balance of power will never shift as dramatically as it may do close to one of the poles. Also, too much weathercock behaviour could easily undermine its actor credibility, a factor being vital to its core strategy of non-commitment.

---

13   The allied powers' abandonment/ entrapment dilemma as formulated by Snyder (1984) will be systematically presented in chapter 7.

14   I do not find it necessary for my purpose to distinguish between various types of alliances (cf. Rothstein 1968). There are, of course, many other 'determinants of choice' regarding alliance posture (Snyder 1984, pp. 471-5) than the one emphasized here. However, as our interest pertains to the occurence of bandwagoning, the seriousness of the threat facing the weak is seen as the most crucial factor. Another factor that might deserve consideration is the level of tension between the ally and the adversary (cf. Mouritzen 1988, pp. 385-9).

To sum up: among the three specific constellations at stake here, I assume bandwagoning to be strongest in the asymmetric constellation, medium (relatively speaking) in the symmetric constellation, and lowest in the alliance constellation.

The apparent effects of the Soviet coup and its aftermath on three weak power foreign policies will be analysed below, one for each of the stipulated constellations. Finland will represent the asymmetric constellation, Sweden the symmetric one and Denmark the alliance constellation. The Finnish and Swedish constellation affiliations were justified in the previous section. Denmark became a NATO alliance member from 1949, as part of a cautious balancing strategy. The Soviet threat facing Denmark during the short period of concern here developed from 'low' to 'low'. In other words not even the few days, where the coup seemed to succeed, led to any significant threat, given the shift in the Central European balance of power that had taken place since about 1988 (the retreat of the Soviet Union from Eastern Europe, notably). In the light of the above reasoning, we should *not* expect Danish bandwagoning in the period[15]. The expectations concerning Finland and Sweden can be established from the constellations, solely. Taken together, hence, we should expect significant bandwagoning on the part of Finland, no such behaviour from Denmark and with Sweden in a middle position. The actual shifts , if any, that took place in each of the three policies, will be confronted with the expectations, and deviations from the expectations will be accounted for by referring to alternative explanatory factors, should such be available.

The policy shifts will be inferred from trend analyses of each of the three weak powers' official statements concerning the coup, their attitudes to the recognition of the Baltic states, their attitudes to EC membership and to the concept of 'neutrality' (Sweden and Finland) and attitude to the 'Friendship, Cooperation and Mutual Assistance Treaty' (FCMA-Treaty) with the Soviet Union (Finland). These were the major issues that were on their agendas

---

15   In fact, Denmark had already bandwagoned the opposite way from 1988, as the threat facing her waned from 'medium' to 'low' in our terms here. Denmark had displayed a marked front-line cautiousness (non-provocation) during the Cold War: no foreign bases or nuclear weapons on Danish territory, special exercise patterns near the island of Bornholm, e.g. As soon as the Red Army had withdrawn from the vicinity of Lübeck to Kaliningrad, however, Denmark could shout her 'real' opinion eastwards on several issues (to be analysed in the present and the following sections). For instance, the Danish reaction to the introduction of Martial law in Poland 1981 was extremely cautious compared to its reactions to the violent events in Lithuania and Latvia in January 1991. The weaker the Soviet Union in Denmark's salient environment, the more anti-Soviet Denmark could act. In other words, Denmark bandwagoned: the Soviet Union was 'punished' by Denmark for being a trend-loser.

during the two weeks at stake. Regarding statements about the coup there were not only declarations by each country, but also an EPC statement (European Political Co-operation) on Tuesday 20 August (the second day of the coup) in the Hague and a common Nordic statement the same day in Skagen (Denmark).

Empirical Trends

We shall now see for each of the three cases, if the trends in their policies can be regarded as bandwagoning or not. As I have chosen to understand this type of behaviour, it is required not only that support for the trend loser is waning (or conversely: the winner is increasingly supported), but also that this happens for pure power (trend) reasons. This is, of course, difficult to prove on the basis of overt materials; still, by comparing diachronic trends in the salient power structure with trends in overt behaviour, I think that reasonable arguments can be provided in one or the other direction.

Trend Interpretation: Finland. Regarding Finnish statements about the coup, the turning point was obviously President Koivisto's press conference on Thursday, i.e. the day after the coup had collapsed. The word 'coup' was used for the first time, and reference was made to the CSCE process. One may ask, of course, why this turning point did not occur on Wednesday evening, when Prime Minister Aho and Foreign Minister Väyrynen talked to the press (Hufvudstadsbladet (Hbl), 22 August), and when it seemed obvious that the coup had failed. However, they may have wished to consult the President before shifting rhetoric and one could, of course, from a cautious point of view wish to 'wait and see' a little further. All things considered, it seems that there was a neat correspondence between the two turning points: the one in the salient power structure and the one in Finnish rhetoric regarding the coup.

As to Baltic independence, the major speeding up occured on Sunday, 25 August. What requires an explanation in this matter is, why publicly declared criteria of recognition like full territorial control and agreements between the Baltic states and the Soviet Union were suddenly abandoned. The timing of this abandoning indicates that not only was Yeltsin's recognition on Saturday important (this was openly admitted by the government). Compared to the other Nordic countries' speeding up, it hints that we are actually dealing with a kind of Nordic race in this question (officially denied, of course, by all governments involved). In the Finnish press, it was actually compared to a bicycle race: the riders lying in wait, carefully watching each other, and one rider suddenly initiating the spurt, trying to take the rest by surprise. Iceland was 'allowed' a lonely spurt already in the spring of 1991, whereas Denmark was not: the others followed closely in her track, making it a close race in the final end. The explanation underlying this race hypothesis clearly involves the Nordic public opinions and their pro-Baltic attitudes. They would hardly allow their respective governments to lag significantly behind the others in the race. Unlike Sweden, there was no upcoming election in Finland, but still it would be troublesome for the government in domestic debate to lag behind the other Nordic governments, especially in view of Finland's historical and linguistic ties to Estonia (cf., e.g., the editorials of Hbl, 27 and 30 August). Another explanation underlying the race hypothesis is probably concern for good future relations with the new independent Baltic states: lagging too much behind the other Nordic countries could be symbolically unfortunate in future dealings with Finland's new neighbours.

This apparent sensibility to public opinion and to future relations with the Baltic states was, however, something entirely new in Finnish foreign (security) policy after 1944. As expressed by President Paasikivi (1946-56), 'Foreign policy is too difficult for the 'man in the street'. The leaders must courageously assume responsibility and guide public opinion' (cf. Mouritzen 1988, p. 322).

Even though a democratization of foreign policy had taken place during President Koivisto's periods in office, the participation in a Nordic popularity race like the one described above would hardly have occured during Finnish adaptive acquiescence – that is, as long as the Soviet Union and the 'old' polarity seemed likely to persist. Finland has traditionally been among the most reluctant states in the Western world in the question of Baltic independence (as opposed to Finnish popular sentiments). In other words, Finland has never allowed herself the freedom of contributing to the likely dissolution of the Soviet empire, through initial support for Baltic independence. However, after the breakdown of the old power structure and with the trend pointing in the direction of the dissolution of the Soviet Union and Baltic independence, anyway, Finland could allow herself to take other considerations into account, including public opinion. It was quite clever to say in the new situation that Finland had never *legally* recognized the Soviet annexation; the fact, however, that this legal circumstance had never been hinted before only serves to indicate the importance of the salient power structure (for a seemingly opposite statement by Koivisto as late as 10 January 1991, cf. p. 71).

Regarding EC-membership, neutrality and the FCMA-treaty, the speeches on 3 September and 4 September represented the most far-reaching shifts ever to occur. As Finland interpreted Soviet views and its neutrality during the old power structure, EC-membership was totally out of the question; Finland had to strive hard for its free trade agreement with the EC and its membership of EFTA (e.g. Hakovirta, 1988)[16]. With the dissolution of the Soviet Union that could be discerned on 3 September and 4 September, not only was 'traditional' EC membership seen as being compatible with neutrality, but possibly also membership in a future political Union with a common security policy. Also, it seems hardly accidental that the first Finnish official statement laying a distance to the military paragraphs of the FCMA-treaty occured so soon after the collapse of the old power structure.

The various 'power interpretations' offered above on a whole range of major issues are mutually supportive: the fact that several crucial turningpoints occured simultaneously, roughly speaking, supports the interpretation that they are caused by one and the same phenomenon: the breakdown of the 'classical' power structure in Finland's salient environment.

The first-mentioned prerequisite for bandwagoning to apply, namely that the apparent trend-winner is increasingly supported (or, conversely, the trend-loser is disfavoured), was also clearly fulfilled in the Finnish case. The initial, extremely cautious rhetoric was replaced by less cautious formulations, as the power trend shifted. Subsequently, as the Soviet Union began to disintegrate, it was 'punished' through Finnish recognition of Baltic independence, the opening of a door to Finnish membership of a Western political Union, the watering down of neutrality and the official 'outdating' of the FCMA-Treaty in its military aspects. We can conclude, hence, that *both* defining characteristics of bandwagoning as here understood have been fulfilled in the case at hand.

In view of our trend focus, various absolute labels are of minor importance. What deserves to be said, though, is that Finland definitely jumped out of adaptive acquiescence during the two weeks that have been considered above. This was the classic foreign policy paradigm that had prevailed since 1944, albeit since the late 1980s in weakened form. The failed coup in the Soviet Union and its aftermath proved to be a forceful injection: firstly, the paradigmatic behaviour was called forward and then, suddenly, its power basis melted away.

---

16   The Finnish version of neutrality implied stricter requirements of symmetry in viewpoints between East and West than the Swedish version. In conflict issues, it often entailed silence (e.g. voting abstentions in the UN). To put it bluntly, one can say that whereas Finnish foreign policy had 'striven for neutrality' in much of the post-war era (an effort not always recognized by the Soviet Union (e.g. Penttilä 1991, ch. 8), it now seemed to be striving *away* from the straitjacket of neutrality (by watering it down).

Trend Interpretation: Sweden. When it comes to Sweden, it should be possible to be more brief, as there are fewer trends to interpret. Regarding official statements about the coup, it can hardly be bandwagoning; quite the contrary. Publicly laying a distance to the common Nordic declaration (a quite unusual thing to do in diplomacy, also hurting the Finns) and declaring that Sweden could have voted for the EC statement (Tuesday during the coup) must have had its strong reasons (cf. below). It was actually tantamount to putting the Swedish weight in the Western scale in the re-established East-West polarity that seemed to exist for a few days. If anything, this amounts to balancing rather than the opposite. There is no trend in this question ; there were no significant amendments later on.

Turning to the recognition of the Baltic states, I have already mentioned the bicycle race metaphor in the above section (along with Yeltsin's recognition that was also crucial for Sweden). Sweden also participated in the bicycle race, and probably for the same reasons as Finland: popular sentiments (even an ongoing election campaign), and concern for a good symbolic platform for future relations with the new Baltic neighbours. Allowing such reasons to play a role in Swedish Baltic policy was, however, far from the traditional course (cf. further pp. 70-1), implying a low profile in the question at the government level. A certain modification occured in connection with the previously mentioned violent events in early 1991, but it was still the Swedish view that independence should be agreed upon between the respective new states and the Soviet Union (together with other requirements). Hence, it was a significant shift of policy that took place on 24 and 25 of August, notably, by joining the race. As expressed in a Swedish editorial (Dagens Nyheter, 28 August): 'Suddenly the principles of international law were irrelevant...The legal strictness has been sacrificed, as politics and emotions have taken over'. The question is, however, if this represents bandwagoning. One prerequisite is clearly fulfilled, in the sense that the trend loser, or what was left of it, was disfavoured by the step. It is an open question, if the other prerequisite is fulfilled: was the rapidly changing power structure part of the explanation, as a necessary condition, or were the above mentioned reasons sufficient? Would they have caused a shift also with a more stable situation in the Soviet Union?

In the question of membership of a future political Union and neutrality, it is impossible to discern any trend whatsoever. Should bandwagoning be involved, Sweden should have laid a distance to its membership application during the coup. This did not occur, as we have seen; quite to the contrary, the membership application was reaffirmed (with continued neutrality). Hence, bandwagoning does not apply here.

To sum up, bandwagoning can *possibly* be found in the Baltic issue. But the opposite type of behaviour occured as regards official statements about the coup.

Trend Interpretation: Denmark. Denmark accompanied its signing of the EPC statement with a range of comments about the coup and its implications: the taking of credit for certain parts of the statement, the teaching of Finland what it should have said, etc. This Danish hyper-activism actually placed Denmark among the 'hawks' as regards Western reactions to the coup. As ironically expressed by the Finnish editor-in-chief Keiho Korhonen (Hbl 24 August): 'Denmark is a Great Power. We can in no way afford what Denmark can'.

Also as regards Baltic independence, we noted a Danish avantgarde position. Denmark did not follow the criteria of international law for recognition, but took a purely political stand. Not only might this help the Baltic states by drawing further recognitions with it (as actually happened), there was also unanimous domestic political support behind this posture. As with declarations about the coup, a purpose may also have been to heighten Denmark's international profile in general, a purpose which seems to have played a role for some years.

This being said, it should be obvious that no bandwagoning can be found in the Danish case. In contrast, balancing was at stake, as Denmark chose to be at the forefront among Western reactions and initiatives from the very beginning. With the military power shifts in Denmark's salient environment from 1988 and the East European revolutions (cf. above), Denmark had bandwagoned so much out of the shadow of the Soviet orbit that a reactionary coup in Moscow led to Danish balancing rather than reverse bandwagoning. Denmark had passed the geopolitical threshold of Soviet influence.

Expectations Confronting Observations

We have expected, on the basis of Baker Fox 'theorizing on small-states' anti-balance of power behaviour and the modifications regarding constellations that have been added here, that Finland would exhibit significant bandwagoning during the period selected for study, that such behaviour would be absent as regards Denmark, and that Sweden would be found in a medium position. How do these expectations relate to what has been observed above (as summarized in fig. 5.1)?

Fig. 5.1 Balancing vs. bandwagoning in Finnish, Swedish and Danish responses to the Soviet disintegration

	Finland	Sweden	Denmark
Statements regarding the coup	Bandwagoning behaviour	Balancing behaviour	Balancing behaviour
Recognition of Baltic independence	Bandwagoning behaviour	Bandwagoning behaviour?	Balancing behaviour
Attitude to EC membership	Bandwagoning behaviour	Unaffected	Irrelevant
Attitude to FCMA-Treaty	Bandwagoning behaviour	Irrelevant	Irrelevant

It should be obvious from the above conclusions that expectations and observations fit neatly in the Finnish and Danish cases. By stipulating *two* criteria of bandwagoning and assuring that both were fulfilled in the Finnish case, I dare say that not only could such behaviour be found superficially (i.e. decreased support to the trend-loser), it was also carried out for the 'right' reason, namely power trend reasons. This, of course, corroborates the theoretical reasoning.

The fit between expectations and observations is more dubious in the Swedish case. Superficially speaking, the Swedish case is 'medium', as there is less bandwagoning than in the Finnish case, and less balancing than in the Danish case, from an aggregate point of view. But it is hardly 'medium' on each of the three issues that have been considered. From the point of view of the credibility of the theoretical reasoning, hence, I should be able to offer reasonable explanations for the deviations that have been found on two of the issues. One explanation, I think, was the ongoing election campaign; parliamentary elections were to be held on 22 September. In view of general popular sentiments, a forceful posture had to be taken vis à vis the Soviet communist coup. If the Skagen declaration had been the only Swedish manifestation, this would unavoidably have been exploited by the bourgeois opposition. The same would have happened, if the government had laid a distance to its EC application. It had been of vital importance to the government's election strategy that a decision on EC membership had been made (late autumn 1990) and that the formal application had been handed over to the EC well before the election (Sundelius 1994). Opinion polls indicated solid pro-EC attitudes among the voters at this time.

Another likely explanation, I think, was concern for the Swedish image in the EC Commission and among EC member-countries. In view of the Swedish application for membership, it was crucial to seem 'mature' and sufficiently 'europeanized' – not least in foreign and security policy issues that would probably be crucial in a future EC Union. This explains, I think, why foreign minister Sten Anderson felt it necessary to take the unusual step of describing what Sweden would have done in a hypothetical situation (i.e. vote for a statement that Sweden had no opportunity to vote for). And it also explains, why it was necessary to stress, almost demonstratively, that the Swedish application was unaffected by events in the Soviet Union.

Sweden had been accused of weathercock behaviour in connection with the EC membership decision in late 1990 (and also previously in this matter, cf. Hakovirta (1988) p. 251). As late as May 1990, the Prime Minister had declared that 'concern for the credibility of our policy of neutrality is the reason why we are not applying for EC membership'. A new revision, this time in the opposite direction, could have undermined Sweden's general credibility both in the EC and among Swedish voters.

Each of these explanations, the EC connection and the election campaign, would, I think, be sufficient to account for the observed deviations. However, the sin of explanatory overkill must be permitted here, where we have access to overt materials, only. The two deviation explanations have, I think, saved the theory from being hurt by the Swedish case. But it has not been really corroborated, either.

The bicycle race explanation, being relevant in all three cases, deserves a few comments. It actually refers to the phenomenon of diffusion, well-known in most segments of social life between the Nordic countries (cf. Karvonen 1981, Nielsson 1990). It should not be seen as an explanation rivalling the status of the balance of power; rather, it served as a catalyst for this more basic explanation, determining, to a large extent, the exact *timing* of bandwagoning behaviour in the Swedish and Finnish cases.

The Danish and Finnish cases have corroborated the theory, as argued above. In particular, the explanatory power of the notion of constellation has been demonstrated (even with such a relatively broad trend-definition of bandwagoning as has been used here). The concept of 'small state' (or 'weak power') is simply too broad to allow for common theory-building.

The always dangerous and insidious sin of circularity is not committed in the present analysis. The theoretical reasonings behind the belief in bandwagoning are based on such general principles as unitary actors or rationality in the face of positive/negative sanctions. Moreover, the empirical inspiration that *may* have played a role for Baker Fox (1959) or Mouritzen (1988), stems from World War II cases, mostly. Hence, the confrontations that have been made here between a theoretically derived hypothesis and empirical observations can hardly express circularity, i.e. that the hypothesis should have been made with the same cases in mind as those that are used in the confrontation.

Nordic Engagements vis à vis the Baltic Countries: A Geopolitical Approach

It is essential to remember that the pre-theory of international politics advocated in this book is hospitable to several specific theoretical constructs. Let us turn to yet another one that is rooted in states' salient environment. In the two former constructs, constellation functioned as parameter; tension between the strong was the independent variable in the first example, and balance of power between them was the independent vaiable in the second example. In this third example location and balance of power still play a role, but a simpler formulation will be made.

The Baltic countries' strivings for independence and later their efforts to become stable Western democracies belonging to Western institutions posed a delicate challenge to the West. The Soviet/Russian conflict with the Baltic countries pertained initially to their sovereign status (Gerner & Hedlund 1993), and later to their borders and the conditions for Russians living in these countries. Although in principle supporting the Baltic cause, Western Great Powers did not want to undermine Gorbachev's and later Yeltsin's domestic positions, both being essential for overall relations with the Soviet Union/ Russia. For the Nordic states, however, assisting the development of these reborn 'small states' in the direction of stable Nordic-Western democracies was actually called for by several factors: the geographical proximity between the Nordic and the Baltic regions, the Nordic countries' small-state ideologies and their traditions of identity promotion (protestant democracy, egalitarianism) abroad – as manifested in their Third World assistances. Moreover, the Nordic tradition of mutual low politics cooperation and its available institutional machinery facilitated Baltic contacts with all five Nordic countries; the Baltic countries were affiliated to the Nordic Council well before their international independences.

This was the lowest common denominator for all five Nordic countries. However, it does not explain the significant *differences* between the five country engagements vis à vis the 'Baltic challenge'. By 'engagement' is simply understood priority given to the challenge in the context of the countries' overall foreign policies. As indicators function diplomatic support for the Baltic countries (as in official statements, for instance) or the offering of practical assistance, be it of a military or low politics nature. In this section we shall postdict the engagements of each of the Nordic countries from a simple geopolitical model (the 'twin distance' model)[17]. We shall then see how that fits the empirical record. The analysis will be divided into a 'before' and 'after' September 1991. Whereas the perspective on the crucial two weeks in August-September was dynamic ('if this *trend* in the salient balance-of-power, then that *trend* in weak power policy'), the perspective here is one of comparative statics: before vs. after September 1991. However, the twin distance model is applied to both phases.

The Twin Distance Model

As shown in the analysis of Nordic reactions to the Soviet disintegration in the previous section, the Cold War constellations got a final renaissance in connection with the failed coup; as we saw, they had considerable explanatory power regarding the reactions of each country at stake. In this section, however, a different (but related) theoretical construct will be applied. For one thing, a longer time perspective is at stake: from the fall of the Berlin Wall 1989 to the present-day, in principle. That makes the Cold War constellations unsuitable as the over-arching perspective. Moreover, the new unipolar EU constellations in Europe have a modest significance for the specific policies at stake here, those in relation to the Baltic countries. Instead, a simpler distance model will be presented and applied.

Each country engagement is seen as the product of an *engagement barrier* and an *engagement incentive*. The former is determined by distance from the Soviet Union/Russia and the latter by distance from the Baltic countries. The propositions as adapted to the case at stake here can be formulated as follows:

(1)   The shorter the distance to the Soviet Union/Russia from a Nordic country, the higher the barrier for its Baltic engagement, and
(2)   The shorter the distance to the Baltic countries from a Nordic country, the higher its incentive for Baltic engagement (cf. fig. 5.2).

---

17   'Postdict' rather than 'predict', since we are dealing with the past (albeit the very recent past).

Engagement barrier should have primacy in relation to engagement incentive until the disintegration of the Soviet Union; after that, the two are expected to carry a roughly equal weighting (to be justified below).

Fig. 5.2 Distances to the Soviet Union/Russia and the Baltic countries from each of the Nordic countries

The reasoning behind proposition (1) is basically that power wanes with distance, and vice versa (Boulding 1962). That means that the closer a country is situated to the Soviet Union/Russia, the more negative sanctions can be projected by Moscow vis à vis this country. (A common border means of course zero distance, although one can in turn differentiate after the length of this common border[18]). Proximity and in particular a common border also means a set of common problems to be solved (pertaining to migration and environment, for instance). That again means unilateral dependency for the weaker party. The more dependency, the more cautious the country in question will behave vis à vis the Soviet Union/Russia. One might object that it would also have an incentive to gamble in order to change the situation (enter a counter-alliance or even contribute to the undermining of the Soviet Union). However, the Soviet Union/Russia were (are) conservative poles in relation to the Nordic countries: they were (are) satisfied with the status quo, just like the Nordic countries themselves. If a Nordic country 'rocked the boat', it might undermine the Soviet/ Russian leadership (Gorbachev/Yeltsin) and pave the way for a reactionary military regime[19]. Such a regime might well be non-status quo oriented.

Baltic international independence represented a grave threat to the Soviet Union, a threat that might undermine the Union as such. In the second period Baltic membership of NATO would be a serious defeat for Russia. The closer a Nordic country within the reach of Soviet/Russian negative sanctions, hence, the more dangerous it would be to interfere in sensitive Soviet 'internal affairs' or tense Russian-Baltic relations. That might undermine the prevailing status quo leadership.

The reasoning behind proposition (2) is that geographical proximity in relation to the Baltic countries entails, ceteris paribus, more common interests in a (future) Baltic Sea region, but also more bilateral common problems and perhaps common history/identities. It should be obvious that the Great Power dependency argument underlying (1) is absent here; instead there is the regional incentive and the opportunity it presents for an influential role to the Nordic country in question. Geographical proximity is measured in the straightforward sense of distance to the nearest Baltic country, but in virtue of the region argument ('Baltic Sea') it will also be understood as the country's Baltic shore length[20].

---

18   Of course, one could differentiate further and consider the location of the country's major industrial and military centres. However, that would complicate the model too much and in any case be irrelevant to the particular countries at stake here.

19   As for the rest of the Western world, the alternative that could be imagined to the status quo was a backlash in the wake of a Soviet military coup; it was *not* the kind of revolution abolishing communism that actually materialized in September 1991.

20   No exact measurement of these variables will be made below, even though that would be possible in principle. I shall limit myself to rough qualitative estimates.

The 1989-91 phase

Geopolitical Expectations. Let us now see, which expectations can be derived from the simple distance model for each of the Nordic countries regarding their Baltic engagements. We shall first analyse the interim period from the fall of the Berlin Wall to the disintegration of the Soviet Union.

For Denmark being close to the Continental European dynamics, the situation had markedly changed with events during late 1989; with the fall of the Berlin Wall, the Central European revolutions and the gradual withdrawal of WAPA troops from the vicinity of Lübeck to Kaliningrad, Denmark was no longer a frontline state. Whereas the Danish status had previously resembled that of Norway, Denmark was now liberated from frontline concerns. The other four Nordic countries were relatively unaffected by the dramatic Central European dynamics. Norway, bordering the Soviet Union in the high North, would as previously have to display frontline cautiousness (the Soviet military concentration in the Kola peninsula, the dispute with the Soviet Union over the Barents Sea economic zones), whereas Iceland in the Atlantic Ocean with the US Keflavik base could live without such concerns. With the 1200 km. common border and the risk of a reactionary coup in Moscow, Finland was asymmetrically placed in the (sleeping) high politics bipolarity[21]. Even though Sweden had no such border, Swedish territorial waters had been a shatterzone between the military blocs through the 1980s. Soviet submarines based on the Baltic coast had regularly violated Swedish territorial integrity during this decade.

Finland and Sweden should have the strongest Baltic proximity incentives, given Finland's proximity to Estonia and Sweden's to all three Baltic countries. As a corollary of this, Finland has strong historical and linguistic ties to Estonia. Moreover, Finland and Sweden have by far the longest Baltic Sea coastlines among the Nordic countries; Sweden attempted during her Great Power period during the 17th and 18th centuries to make the Baltic a Swedish domestic sea. Denmark is further away from the Baltic countries and has no corresponding historical affinities. However, her traditional function as plug in the Baltic Sea and communication gateway to the Continent sounded promising in relation to a future Baltic Sea region. Even less proximate are Norway, not to speak of Iceland. None of these countries have Baltic Sea shores.

---

21   The distinction between high and low politics will be discussed extensively pp. 121-3. The sphere of general relationships between states ('general diplomacy') will always be high politics during anarchy, whereas substantial spheres will normally belong to low politics (though not necessarily so).

However, engagement incentive should be a clearly subordinate factor in relation to engagement barrier during the interim period. The barrier *allowed* the incentive to play a role for some countries, but not for others. Relations with a nearby superpower or great power, with a different ideological orientation, would at any time supersede considerations pertaining to (future) relations with some as yet non-recognized states.

Fig. 5.3 Nordic engagements for the Baltic cause 1989-91 as expected from the twin distance model

	Soviet proximity/ border concern	Baltic proximity incentive	Expected engagement for the Baltic cause
1. Denmark	no	yes	strong
2. Iceland	no	no	medium(?)
3. Sweden	yes	yes	medium/modest
4. Finland	yes(!)	yes	modest
5. Norway	yes	no	modest

Filling in fig. 5.3, it should be clear how much we expect each of the Nordic countries to engage in the Baltic cause during the interim period. Denmark with virtually no Soviet concern and the prospects for participating in a future Baltic region should be motivated the most. Norway scoring opposite at the two dimensions should be at the bottom. For both Sweden and Finland the dimensions push in opposite directions; with primacy to the great power dimension, however, the two countries' engagements should be expected to be modest. Sweden with no common border with the Soviet Union should be expected to display a somewhat higher profile than Finland, though. For Iceland, no dilemma like the Swedish or Finnish ones would be present; Soviet sensitivities could be disregarded, but on the other hand there would not be much self-interest in a high profile, either. A medium profile should be expected, but with considerable freedom of action.

The empirical record.   From 1989, markedly, the Danish government encouraged non-governmental contacts between *Denmark* and the Baltic countries (circumscribing the Soviet authorities). Culture could be used as a convenient excuse also for high politics contacts, as illustrated by the opening of a Danish Culture Institute in Riga in 1990. Denmark took every opportunity to create international attention and support for the Baltic cause. The free multi-party elections in the Baltic countries in March and April 1990 and the countries' formal declarations of independence were welcomed; however, no official recognitions were made, since Moscow still exerted real authority in their territories[22]. Visits of Parliamentary presidiums and delegations and Prime and Foreign Ministers took place, although the Danish Foreign Minister did not travel to the Baltic countries before he could do so without a Soviet visa (Hoppe 1994 p. 80). Denmark was the first country to propose that the Balts should be grouped along with the new Central and East European democracies regarding assistance for their economic transitions. As the Baltic countries could not get observer status at the CSCE conference in November 1990, for instance, Denmark assisted them in arranging an informal press conference outside the conference hall. Inside the hall, Denmark presented the sharpest formulations in support of Baltic international independence (along with Iceland). In December 1990 a Baltic information office was opened in Copenhagen; the occasion was celebrated by the presence of all Nordic and Baltic Foreign Ministers (the formulation of a joint Nordic communiqué in support of the Balts was attempted, but failed; cf. Ozolina 1996 p. 96). The violent events in Vilnius and Riga in January 1991 were sharply condemned by Denmark; shortly thereafter co-operation protocols between Denmark and each of the Baltic countries were signed, expressing the wish for early re-establishments of diplomatic relations between the countries (i.e. the relations that had been broken off with the Soviet occupation in 1940). The signing of these protocols was described as an 'unfriendly act' by the Soviet government (Hoppe 1994 p. 82).

In spite of a meagre resource base, *Iceland* manoeuvred herself into an avantgarde position. Iceland recognized Lithuanian independence on 11 February 1991 and declared that diplomatic relations would be established, thereby even superseding the Danes (Jonson 1991 p. 135). The Soviet Union withdrew her ambassador from Reykjavik in response. Iceland also supported the Baltic countries in the UN and the CSCE contexts. Naturally, however, it was impossible for Icelandic diplomacy to rival the rest of the Danish efforts described above.

Whereas Denmark, Norway and Iceland had not recognized the Soviet annexations of the Baltic countries in July 1940 (they were themselves not free at the time and were therefore not tempted to do it), Sweden and Finland had done so – probably for simple geopolitical reasons. *Sweden* had hosted

---

22 Whereas Lithuania demanded outright independence, the Estonian and Latvian declarations spoke of a period of transition (Ozolina 1996 p. 94).

strong Baltic exile organizations since World War II, and popular sympathies for the Baltic countries were strong and less amorphous than in Denmark. However, relations with the nearby superpower were more important at the level of government; Sweden could not afford to join the Danes in their anti-Soviet needle pricking. The violent events in January 1991 led to a heightened Swedish tone in favour of Baltic independence (Samuelsson 1996 pp. 23-9); still, caution persisted in high politics until the bicycle race in August 1991 described in the previous section. In low politics, however, Sweden was at least as active as Denmark, initiating the largest program of assistance among the Nordic countries.

In spite of the lack of historical ties, there were almost the same pro-Baltic attitudes at the parliamentary and the grassroot levels in *Norway* as in the other Nordic countries. Norway expressed much goodwill for the Baltic cause within a Nordic institutional framework. However, the Norwegian government consistently followed a low profile course, as the yearnings for independence got momentum in the Baltic republics. As Lithuania had declared itself independent in March 1990, Norway declined a request from Lithuania to supply it with oil during the subsequent Soviet economic boycott (Knudsen 1996 p. 117).

This 'Lithuanian crisis' also brought the Finnish dilemma to a peak; no agreement at a meeting of Nordic foreign ministers in Copenhagen in April could be achieved (Ozolina 1996 p. 97). The violent events in Vilnius and Riga in January 1991 likewise presented a difficult situation for *Finland;* however, it was obvious that the Soviet vector proved axiomatic once again:

> We do not interfere in Soviet internal matters. Finland has recognized that the Baltic countries belong to the Soviet Union, and we stick to all international agreements...We have also supported the view that in particular a small country should see to it that its friends are close at hand; if one must necessarily have enemies, they should be far away...There is reason to stress that also Finland has its own interests, and it is also a moral question to safeguard Finland's own interests... Living in an unstable world where emotions are volatile, it is in my opinion important that we don't provoke people to enter a path where we are not prepared to follow them (president Koivisto, meeting with journalists, 10 January 1991, Koivisto 1992).

Finland's special concern for her Soviet relations – as in the above quotations, e.g. – sometimes led to criticism for amorality in the West (the Finlandization theme). This in turn led to Finnish counter-attacks,

Sometimes we have special difficulties in finding a common line with the Nordic countries. That is because that they in our opinion are very quick to make decisions and that this is done in a more emotional way than is common internationally [referring to the Nordic 'bicycle race' regarding the recognition of the Baltic countries]....One could say that we in that respect are typical Lutherans, that we always have a bad conscience. Sometimes it is implied in the West that it is our fault that we are not more numerous than we are. It is our fault that we have lost wars instead of winning them. And it is our fault that our geographical location is what it is, that we for instance are not an island in the middle of a sea. However, we have tried to find solutions to our problems from our own preconditions (president Koivisto, interview in Estonian radio and television, 6 September 1991; Koivisto 1992).

It seems that the five country postdictions fit with the empirical record, roughly speaking. The only minor discrepancy is Iceland's rivalling the Danish avantgarde position by actually being first to recognize Lithuanian independence. Possibly the memory of Iceland's own recent independence (1944) has played a role in this question. Apart from this instance, however, there is no need to search for alternative explanatory factors at systemic/ regional or internal political levels. Neither would such a search be succesful, given the identical systemic/ regional contexts that the countries were located in, and given their roughly similar domestic societies and decision-making procedures.

The post-1991 period

Geopolitical Expectations. Even though not the only causes, the international recognitions of the Baltic countries in September 1991 set in motion self-reinforcing processes that before the end of the year had contributed to the dissolution of the Soviet Union (Gerner & Hedlund 1993). This entailed a profound revision of the power structure in the salient environments of Finland and Sweden among the countries being considered here. Combined with the international independences of the three Baltic countries, new opportunities presented themselves for the Baltic profiles of the Nordic countries – but of more revolutionary natures for some than for others.

With the unpredictable situation in Russia and the issues of contention between Russia and the reborn Baltic states, the two geopolitical dimensions used above can be reapplied. However, 'Russia proximity' did not by far mean the same as 'Soviet proximity' had done, given Russia's inward-orientation and the disappearance of communism; therefore, there was not the kind of hierarchy between the two dimensions that had existed during the previous period. The transformation on the great power dimension meant very little to Denmark and Iceland who had already disregarded Soviet/Russian sensitivities previously; Norway's neighbour issues in relation to Russia were practically the same as before. The implications were obvious, however, for Finland and Sweden; Sweden could now disregard Russia almost as much as Denmark, and Finland's Russia relations did in no way have the primacy that the Soviet relations had. As interpreted in the previous section, this was 'anti-balance of power' or bandwagoning behaviour (Baker Fox 1959): support the winning side or, as here, turn your back on the losing side in a Great Power contest (thereby in essence repeating the Danish behaviour from 1988).

The Baltic proximity dimension was stronger than before, since the Baltic states had now undeniably regained their independence and a true Baltic Sea region was no longer wishful thinking. The ranking should be as analysed in connection with the interim period; Sweden and Finland followed by Denmark should have the strongest Baltic proximity incentives.

Which postdictions can be made on this twin geopolitical basis (cf. fig.5.4), then? Sweden should now be on top, having a slight lead in relation to Denmark thanks to her strong proximity incentives. Finland should lag a little behind the two; her extensive Russia border and the cool Estonia-Russia relations should induce her to a more cautious posture and present a delicate dilemma in relation to her close Estonia ties. Iceland being unconstrained by any such vectors would have a medium profile (but again rather unpredictable), whereas Norway would continue to be modestly engaged for the same reasons as previously.

Fig. 5.4   Nordic engagements for the Baltic cause post-1991 as expected from the twin distance model

	Russian proximity/ border concern	Baltic proximity incentive	Expected engagement for the Baltic cause
1. Sweden	no	yes!	strong!
2. Denmark	no	yes	strong
3. Finland	yes	yes	medium
4. Iceland	no	no	medium (?)
5. Norway	yes	no	modest

The empirical record. The Baltic countries almost literally turned their backs on Russia after independence, for instance by refusing membership in the CIS and reacting strongly against being mentioned as part of the Russian 'near abroad'. Priority no.1 was to get the former Soviet troops to leave their territories (achieved 1993-94). The three countries saw themselves as 'West' and stretched out for membership in the EU, NATO and other Western organizations. As major Western powers would not let Baltic problems 'rock the boat' in relation to Russia, and as Germany was moreover preoccupied with her own unification process and relations with the Visegrad countries (and inhibited by her past, presumably), Denmark, Sweden and Finland became the Western countries giving highest priority to the Balts (e.g. Tunander 1996 p. 273). These three were also seen by most Western countries as those who should take 'responsibility' for the time being, given the problems or in any case delays with Baltic EU and NATO memberships.

Sweden took on a role of special regional responsibility during Carl Bildt. Although all Nordic countries made statements to the effect that the former Soviet troops should leave the Baltic territories, Sweden was probably the most effective as Bildt managed to make Clinton take up the issue with Yeltsin. Sweden turned somewhat away from the region during Ingvar Carlsson from 1994. As Göran Persson entered office in the spring of 1996, however, the responsibility role ('the Baltic cause is ours') was resumed in full understanding with the US administration; the visit of Göran Persson to the White House was important in this regard (Vikström 1996; cf.also Asmus and Nurick 1996). This role was whole-heartedly taken on by Sweden except for the shouldering of security commitments.

Denmark had an advantage over Sweden by being a NATO member, a status strongly desired by the Baltic countries. This gave Denmark the highest military profile in the region. Denmark was first to integrate Baltic platoons into her battalions in Croatia and in Bosnia (IFOR). Denmark managed to get the 'Baltic region countries' mentioned in the NATO summit communiqué 1997 (along with Slovenia and Rumania) and was applauded for that by the Balts. President Clinton's visit to Copenhagen in the summer of 1997 was interpreted as a US recognition of Denmark's Baltic engagement, inter alia.

Finland holds a lower profile in the Baltic sphere regarding high politics (at least officially), but Finland's linguistic-cultural and rapidly developing economic ties to Estonia are unique. Actually, Finland advocates a country-specific approach, according to which each Nordic-Western country should take 'responsibility' for only one Baltic country – Estonia in the case of Finland obviously. However, such an approach has been discarded by Denmark, Sweden, and Norway.

Norway holds a markedly lower profile than that of the leading trojka. Barents cooperation in the North is explicitly given higher priority than the Baltic Sea region (Foreign Minister Godal 30 January 1997). Given the specific stakes that Norway has vis à vis Russia in the North (oil, fish, nuclear waste, inter alia), Norway follows a clear 'Russia first' course. There is no reason to offend Russia 'unnecessarily' in the Baltic Sea area, if that has a price in the North. This means stricter limits regarding the rather modest defence co-operation than for the other Nordic countries. One should bear in mind also that Norway approaches the Baltic area with a NATO badge, but without an EU badge; that means that Russian sensitivities are likely to be more serious than in the case of Denmark carrying both badges (the EU being uncontroversial to Russia). Norway avoids emphasizing the issue of Baltic NATO membership in official statements (unlike Denmark and Iceland), and enthusiasm for NATO enlargement as such has cooled down remarkably in the wake of Russian protests (Kjølberg 1996 p. 338). By contrast, almost demonstrative weight is laid on consideration for Russia: 'Russia's legitimate security interests must be taken into account [in NATO's adaptation process]...Russia is in virtue of her size and importance NATO's most important co-operation partner' (Foreign Minister Godal 30 January 1997).

Norway has managed to engage Sweden and Finland as well as the EU Commission in the Barents region, so as to avoid too much bilateral dealings with the Russian Great Power. This is the hidden agenda for the Barents initiative. However, that means that Norway must make *some* effort in the Baltic countries (as in BALTBAT, the Baltic peace-keeping Batallion), as a *quid pro quo* for other countries' interest in the Barents region (e.g. Jervell 1996 p. 8).

In fact, visits to the Baltic countries from Nordic Prime Ministers provide an indicator of priorities: for instance, the Norwegian Prime Minister visited the Baltic countries early 1996 about two years after visits by her Nordic colleagues (Knudsen 1996 p. 127).

Norway's priority given to the Third World in comparison to the Baltic Sea region appears from her offering 300 million Norwegian crowns to Tanzania in 1995 compared to 50 millions to the three Baltic countries the same year (Kjølberg 1996 p. 336).

Iceland has naturally fallen behind due to her limited resource base, but selected initiatives like assisting the Estonians with the establishment of an ombudsman institution could be emphasized. As to high politics, Iceland has followed up on her avantgarde position; as expressed by foreign minister Asgrimsson:

> ...all applying states should be offered membership simultaneously, but progress should depend on membership talks. This view is based not least on the interests of the Baltic states, as it is our declared policy to support their membership in the first round (speech in Parliament (Althingi) 17 April 1997).

> It would be totally unacceptable if certain countries were to be defined as not being eligible for NATO membership. In this context I would like to draw your attention to the case of the Baltic States and ask that their needs and aspirations receive your goodwill and attention (speech at the meeting of the Standing Committee of the North Atlantic Assembly, Reykjavik, 5 April 1997).

Only Iceland and Denmark support Baltic NATO membership in the first round among current members[23].

A comparative indicator of Baltic profile is provided by financial assistance level: Sweden is followed by Denmark, Finland follows thereafter, while Norway falls far behind[24]. In other words, Sweden has taken the lead outside high politics, whereas Norway falls markedly behind the leadership trojka.

From an aggregate point of view, Denmark, Sweden, and Finland constitute a top trojka, with Finland a little behind the two others. Distinguishing according to target country, however, Denmark and Sweden have taken a clear lead regarding Latvia and Lithuania, whereas we see a full-fledged trojka regarding Estonia.

Co-operation/Rivalry.   With this leadership duo/trojka in Baltic assistance, both cooperation and rivalry developed between them, thereby adding to the basic geopolitical impetus. Evidently, the fact that each of the two/three could

---

23   Not being members, Sweden and Finland have not found it proper to state an opinion in this matter. Instead, and together with Denmark, they have warmly recommended the EU 'soft security' to the Balts and worked for Baltic EU memberships.

24   Iceland is beyond comparison, of course. There are about as many ways of measuring assistance level as there are measurements. In the period 1990-94, Sweden offered 2700 million Norwegian kr. to the three Baltic countries, Denmark offered 580, Finland 500 and Norway 70 (Kjølberg 1996 p. 336). According to the Danish Foreign Ministry, Sweden and Denmark offered both around 490 million Danish kr. in 1995, Finland 130 and Norway 60.

foresee that also others would display a high profile meant that the task did not seem unrealistic and unmanageable. This was an encouragement, evidently, to make an extra effort oneself. Co-operation to solve the common task could be expected.

Turning to the rivalry side, however, there was competition to get at least as much credit for the effort as the others involved, preferably even more (competition for credit being always of a zero-sum nature). Also this side of the coin functioned as catalyst for an extra effort, and in particular for *visible* efforts. There was surely a good deal of prestige in being Nordic/world avant-garde (with Iceland) in the recognition of the Baltic states, as appears from public statements by the then Danish foreign minister (Ellemann-Jensen) – in particular being ahead of Sweden[25]. This initial rivalry has been repeated in subsequent, less visible matters. Denmark and Sweden seem to be competing for the attention of the Clinton administration. During August 1996, there was semi-public rivalry between Sweden and Finland – won by Persson – concerning whose 'Baltic Commission' should prevail (Hbl 30 August 1996)[26]; Sweden has taken too visible a lead according to certain Finnish ministers (Hbl 12 November 1996). In December 1996, the Finnish Prime Minister Lipponen came out with some harsh words against 'helpful advisors' with questionable motives (Dagens Nyheter 4 December 1996): 'some are directly misguiding the Balts and wish to appear as better than others, as they support Baltic NATO membership'. It is not difficult to see Copenhagen as the main target of these remarks. In January 1997, opposition leader Ellemann-Jensen blamed the Danish government for letting Sweden take the lead in the Baltic Sea region. The secretariat function of the Council of Baltic Sea States (CBSS) is being provided by Persson's Baltic Commission; if a CBSS secretariat could not be located in Copenhagen ('where it naturally belongs'), it would be preferable to have it in Tallinn – if that could prevent rivalling Stockholm from retaining it (Ugebrevet Mandag Morgen, 3 February, 1997 p. 24). In any case, the competition at stake in the parallel action sphere urges each country not to fall behind the others and preferably even do a little bit more. This has entailed that the top trojka has widened the distance to Norway and Iceland.

---

25   As shown in the previous section, the rivalry explanation was perhaps even more powerful the other way round. In spite of remaining high politics concerns in relation to the Soviet Union, it was essential for mainly domestic political reasons for Sweden and Finland to try to catch up with Denmark/Iceland in the 'bicycle race' that developed.

26   In actual fact, this strife was of a domestic nature in both Sweden and Finland (the governmental vs. the non-governmental level), but it came to appear in the press as a national competition between the two countries.

Explaining Much by Little ?

How does the empirical record fit the geopolitically based expectations? The basic pattern consisting of a top trojka and Norway at the bottom fits very well, indeed; Iceland has continued her avantgarde positions at the diplomatic level, but for resource reasons her practical efforts are not comparable to those of the other countries. The postdiction that Sweden should have taken over the yellow bicycle shirt is confirmed regarding the sheer volume of specific assistance; that is even more remarkable in view of Sweden's economic crisis during the 1990s. However, the fact that Denmark is still able to rival Sweden regarding the position as aggregate 'regional leader' requires a specific supplementary explanation outside the distance model: the heritage from the Cold War pattern of constellations. NATO has managed to survive, and survive well, in the absence of her previous enemy. The Great Powers holding a low profile as described above and Norway engaging herself so modestly in the Baltic area for the reasons indicated by the distance model, Denmark has been able to exploit her NATO prestige to its fullest extent in the area. Closely connected to this is a possible role as US errand boy in the area (and elsewhere). It may have become apparent to the US administration that Denmark's activism can serve US interests (Heurlin 1995). How much of Danish activism expresses anticipation of US preferences and how much is independent from such considerations is, however, a question that is difficult to answer with any clarity. There are indications that the causal impetus may be the *reverse:* Denmark seeking to push the US and other major NATO countries into military co-operation with the Baltic countries[27]. Danish defence co-operation with Central Asian republics, for instance, beyond Denmark's own obvious interests may be a *quid pro quo* in order to safeguard US engagement in the Baltic sphere. The NATO connection can probably also explain, why Denmark rather than Sweden got a Clinton visit during 1997, thereby calling the Swedish regional leadership position in question (roughly estimated). At a practical level, existing NATO infrastructure (the Karup airbase) and US support seemed to give Denmark the PfP Headquarter instead of Sweden (Gotland had been suggested).

Apart from this constellation heritage that tends to sharpen the very top competition, it is striking how much can be accounted for by the parsimonious, if not primitive, twin distance model (explaining much by little!). It is possible to postdict five countries' engagement rank order both before and after the

---

27   Cf. *Rapport om dansk Baltikum-politik,* Danish Foreign Ministry 30 September 1996.

Soviet disintegration, without the least recourse to systemic polarity, regional polarity, domestic politics, decision-making or idiosyncratic factors[28]. Governments' party colours, for instance, were unimportant.

---

28 The only (slight) exception seems to have been the Ingvar Carlsson/Göran Persson difference, probably rooted in a generational difference within the Social Democratic party (Carlsson sharing the Cold War heritage). Cf. also Archer (1997) pp. 82-4.

6 Salient Environment and Domestic Explanatory Factors: The Nature of the Interplay

We have seen that a system of non-mobile units like international politics favours salient environment at the expense of systemic explanation of unit behaviour. Three specific theoretical constructs following these lines have been tested. With minor exceptions, these theoretical constructs were not complicated by *unit-internal* sources of behaviour. What does non-mobility or other circumstances/ mechanisms entail for the role of these sources of foreign policy, we should now ask? In particular, what is the nature of their interplay with the salient environment factors and what role, if any, should they be alotted in theory-building?

Levels of Explanation: Complementarism vs. Supplementarism

Ever since the 'level of analysis' theme was launched in IR by Singer (1961), there has been disagreement not only regarding which levels should be singled out, but also as to the more fundamental question of the *relationship* among these levels: can, for instance, factors belonging to different levels be combined in one explanation – or should each level be seen as self-sufficient? According to the latter view – that I label 'complementarism' – one can explain on the basis of one level or another, but each level is seen as producing a full explanation (example: Allison 1971). According to the former view – that I label 'supplementarism' – an explanation based on one specific level can be somehow supplemented with factors belonging to other levels, if it cannot in itself account satisfactorily for what it set out to explain (example: Wolfers 1962)[1].

Which should be preferred, then, supplementarism or complementarism? There is no straight answer to this question. It depends on one's metaphysical conviction. I shall argue (pp. 151-3) that supplementarism follows logically

---

1   Singer (1961) might seem to be a complementarist, as his systemic and his subsystemic levels cannot be combined in one single explanation. This is, however, due to the fact that he sees the subsystemic level as the most suitable locus of explanation, proper (vs. description or prediction). Therefore, there is not much to combine it with, for obvious reasons.

from metaphysical realism, whereas complementarism follows from metaphysical idealism/relativism. Since this book is committed to metaphysical realism, a supplementarist position will be taken. In other words, factors from different levels *can* be combined in specific explanations, if that is what reality calls for (cf. also pp. 6-7 and 147 on the stepwise abandoning of simplifying assumptions). The question for the moment is just *how* they can be combined.

The House on Fire

Anyone with a minimum of familiarity with international politics knows that internal factors may sometimes be co-determinants of foreign policy; the question is just when and how, and how such an insight may be coupled to theories stressing units' salient environment. We need not only a distinct conception of the interplay between external and internal factors (encompassing both the domestic and decision-making levels), but also theoretically grounded *reasons* for such a conception.

Goldmann (1976) presents three models of interplay between internal and 'foreign sources of foreign policy': an additive model, a requisite model and an information model (fig.6.1)[2]. The requisite model (here: 'control-relax model') is the one that I have chosen as the most suitable one. Its principle is that internal factors affect foreign policy only when the external environment 'allows' it. External factors influence the *relation* between internal factors and foreign policy. In the additive model the internal factors function independently from the external ones and the two sets of causal powers (on an equal footing) are therefore amenable to simple addition. In the control-relax model, by contrast, the role of internal determinants *cannot* be understood without a consideration of external factors (whereas these can be understood on their own). It may actually be the case that internal factors do play a major role as efficient causes – but only if 'permitted' by the external environment (the permissive cause)[3]. This metaphorical shorthand formulation requires

---

2   It is telling for asymmetrical US-European relations in IR that one can publish on the topic for Goldmann's article, for instance, in the US without referring to it. Cumulation suffers as crucial distinctions or good ideas in general have to be reinvented in the US perhaps a decade or so after they have been published in Europe. Shortly after such a reinvention, however, they will be enthusiastically received in Europe as 'new wisdom'. Of course there are exceptions to any rule, but this is the general pattern that could be illustrated by several examples.

3   It should be emphasized that the most basic environment factors (like constellations, e.g.) may perform their 'control function' also vis à vis other environment factors.

Fig. 6.1 Three models of interplay between external and internal foreign policy determinants (adapted from Goldmann)

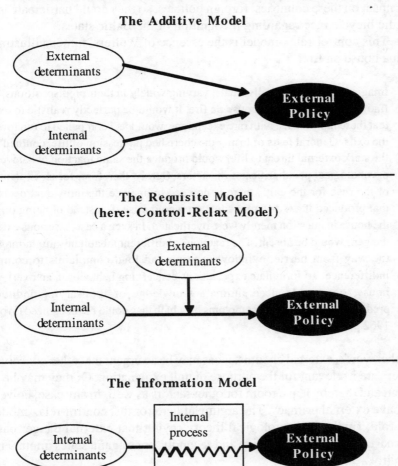

The Additive Model

The Requisite Model
(here: Control-Relax Model)

The Information Model

more precision, of course: in the light of external circumstances, the unit leadership may wish and manage to control internal factors (unit subgroups), or it may relax and allow them to function more or less freely. This is not the whole story, however: subgroups will be easier to control in case of external danger, both because of their voluntary cohesion *and* their anticipated reaction of measures from the leadership.

We have already seen a modest example of such interplay in chapter 5:

with unmistakable signs of the coming dissolution of the Soviet Union, pro-Baltic attitudes in the Finnish and Swedish populations were *allowed* to have an impact on these countries' foreign policies, so they could participate in the Nordic bicycle race regarding recognition of the Baltic states.

This control-relax model is the essence of Wolfers' famous illustration with a house on fire:

> Imagine a number of individuals, varying widely in their predispositions, who find themselves inside a house on fire. It would be perfectly realistic to expect that these individuals, with rare exceptions, would feel compelled to run towards the exits. General fears of losing the cherished possession of life, coupled with the stark external threat to life, would produce the same reaction, whatever the psychological peculiarities of the actors. Surely, therefore, for an explanation of the rush for the exits, there is no need to analyze the individual decisions that produced it...A different situation would arise if, instead of being on fire, the house in question merely were overheated. In such a case, ...serious external danger...would be absent. The reactions of different inhabitants might range all the way from hurried window-opening and loud complaints to complete indifference. To formulate expectations concerning behavior in an overheated house, one would need intimate knowledge of the varying individual predispositions and of the symptoms by which they could be recognized (Wolfers 1962 pp. 13-14).

In other words, external circumstances may be so urgent that other conceivable factors are irrelevant for the purpose of unit explanation. Or they may be less urgent and thereby leave room for other factors as well. In any case, however, we have external primacy. The argument here for this control-relax model is two-fold: firstly the sociological theory saying that external danger causes internal cohesion/centralization and secondly, once again, states' mutual non-mobility.

External Danger/Internal Cohesion-Centralization

The study of social conflict was revived in sociological theory during the 1950s, in particular with Lewis Coser's book 'The Functions of Social Conflict' (1956). Its errand was to reconstruct the conflict theory of the German sociologist Georg Simmel, as formulated in 'Der Streit' (1904), through Coser's own conceptual efforts and in the light of a semi-century of empirical research[4]. External danger (conflict)/internal cohesion-centralization is 'perhaps the best-known and most widely accepted hypothesis in social science' (Sylvan and Glassner, 1985, p. 18), even though the necessary specifications are not always mentioned; in the words of Dahrendorf, 'it appears to be a general law that human groups react to external pressure by increased internal coherence' (cited from ibid). The link between external danger and internal cohesion-centralization is not just a hypothesis or proposition; together with its underlying set of reasons, it constitutes a theory. Moreover, the fact that this theory has been supported empirically at widely different levels of aggregation means that it has acquired a good deal of corroboration: from inter-personal relations to small-groups, organizations, nation-states and nation-state alliances. The relevant research within various disciplines and also across disciplinary boundaries constitutes a process of cumulation that is quite impressive compared to the normal pattern in sociology or political science/international relations.

The theory is applied here to the national level (Mouritzen 1997b). The more manifest the external danger[5], the more curb is laid on internal factors. This may be enforced from above (centralization of decision-making at all levels of government), it may express anticipated reaction (e.g. self censorship in the press, cohesion among regime supporting political parties), or it may exhibit a more spontaneous character (e.g. popular support for the government). The enforcement from above and the anticipated reaction imply infringements on the unit's democratic character (if it was there in the first place).

To mention a few research results from national decision-making, centralization during crisis (i.e. substituting 'level of conflict'/'crisis' for 'danger') has been corroborated empirically[6]. As expressed by Hermann (1969),

---

4   'Coser's strongest theme', LeVine and Campbell (1972, p. 31); it has also been labeled the 'in-group/out-group hypothesis' (cf. Levy, 1989b, p. 260).

5   I shall consistently use 'danger' rather than 'conflict' as the proper independent variable. One can think of 'imperialist' conflict that does not present significant danger to the nation-state (unit) itself. As marginal rather than core values are at stake, it is questionable whether this kind of conflict will produce the urgency being necessary for much internal cohesion to emerge. Secondly, the pursuit of marginal values involves a wider freedom of action than does the defence of a core value like one's own autonomy; there are more types of marginal values that one can choose to pursue – in several geographical directions – and further possible strategies to follow in the process. This makes the soil fertile for discord among various domestic groupings (Mouritzen 1997b pp. 11-12).

6   Cf., e.g., Berelson and Steiner (1964, p. 370); Buchan (1966, pp. 40-1); Hermann (1969, chs. 6,7); Hermann (1972, pp. 196-98); McGowan and Shapiro (1973, proposition 9); Karvonen (1984) notably p. 137; Goldmann et.al. (1986, p. 21).

In crisis as compared to non-crisis, the number of decision makers exercising authority in the decision process is decreased; that is, a contraction of authority occurs (p. 161)...The contraction hypothesis is probably the most widely reported proposition about the effects of crisis (p. 163).

Posen (1984) investigates the relative merits of balance of power theory and organization theory (studying military bureaucracies) for the explanation of national military doctrine:

> Under what conditions will organization theory enjoy its greatest explanatory power? Under what conditions will the international environment have the greatest influence? In times of relative international calm we should expect a high degree of organizational determinism [importance of military bureaucracies and their mutual competition, HM]. In times of threat we should see greater accomodation of doctrine to the international system... (Posen 1984 p. 80).

Regarding political parties, mutual cohesion during national crises is a well-known phenomenon, as illustrated by the formation of 'wall-to-wall' coalition governments when war occurs or appears imminent (Stein, 1976, pp. 164-5).

Theoretical Justification.   The specific *reasoning* behind the proposition at stake here is simply that the curtailment of subunits' autonomy is an extra power resource (increased self-control) that the national regime[7] can mobilize in the face of danger, in order to add to its own autonomy (defensive power). The opportunity for outside forces to play off different subunits against each other *(divide et impera,* divide and rule) will be reduced, as a more coherent facade can be presented vis à vis the external world. That is, the possibility for an outsider to offer strategic rewards to specific subunits, or penetrate the regime in other ways, is reduced or eliminated[8]. Note that an actor's autonomy

---

7   The national actor is conceptualized in this book as a 'regime', as defined p. 32. For reasons of variance, I allow myself a shifting vocabulary for this concept, if the differences are unimportant. In the present chapter, however, it is theoretically crucial to stick strictly to 'regime', since it makes a difference to the 'state', for instance.

8   The extreme case of such penetration happens, if the external power manages to make the regime rulers 'compromise themselves' in the eyes of the population majority. In that case it is unlikely that they will be restrained in the future by public opinion; their possibility to re-establish a respectable image will be minimal, anyway. Their prime concern will be to stay in power by virtue of the external power's goodwill (a 'puppet regime'). That will probably require further 'compromising behaviour'.

(its ability to avoid external actors' influence) and its self-control (the curtailment of its subunits' autonomies) are two different concepts that should not be confused. But they are certainly empirically related, as the main reasoning underlying the proposition should illustrate: the better an actor's self-control, the easier it is to avoid subunits being played off against each other by external forces and the better, consequently, will be its ability to withstand external pressure[9].

This being the basic mechanism behind the mobilization of self-control in the face of danger, it should be added that the regime leadership's vested *interests* domestically in such a mobilization is likely to reinforce it. If a danger really exists and increases, it is unlikely that rulers should miss the opportunity to improve their power position internally through (over)—centralization and an extra bit of cohesion encouragement.

It might be objected that a government may reap advantage externally from internal conflict, provided that the government is closer to the source of external danger than the opposition (Mouritzen 1997b pp. 17-8). This is 'fundamentalist' opposition in the sense that it takes regime values more seriously than the government. Paradoxically as it may sound, it may be useful to the government if such an opposition has certain assets at its disposal, be it voting power or 'chaos power'. This will increase the government's credibility externally, when stressing its regime values (Yeltsin has exploited this vis à vis the West, for instance). This is an insight from game theory ('chicken game'): limited freedom of action in one direction may be an asset in another direction (Schelling 1980 p. 27). Of course, once such an opposition exists a government will exploit the tactical benefits that can be reaped externally from the situation. However, the point here is that no government would consciously run the risk of encouraging such a precarious balance. It might sow the seeds of its own subversion.

As to the more specific mechanisms underlying the mobilization of self-control, the autonomy of bureaucratic subunits (e.g. ministries for specific issue-areas) regarding their contacts abroad will be increasingly curtailed by a central agency. That may be, e.g., the Prime Minister's Office or the Foreign

---

9   One could illustrate autonomy at different organization/group levels (like a Chinese box system) in the following way: as the autonomy of one organization/group is threatened from outside, its self-control is improved by the curtailment of the autonomies of its sub-organizations/groups (be it voluntary or enforced). These, in turn, take corresponding measures towards their respective *sub*-organizations/groups, and so on. In this way, a wave of self-control can flow downwards through a Chinese box system. Conversely, the removal of the top external threat will probably push the wave back again, as sub-units reassert themselves at one level after the other.

Ministry, claiming to monopolize both the breadth of view and the professional diplomatic skill that is in extra demand in a situation of manifest external danger (e.g. Karvonen & Sundelius, 1987, p. 112; Mouritzen, 1988, ch. 22). Ministries of Agriculture or Environment, for instance, will be increasingly subordinated to co-ordination and control in times of external danger, so as to prevent them from pursuing their own sector 'foreign policies'.

Moreover, regarding those subunits with a specific potential to affect others – the press, notably – measures will be taken to make them act like a kind of co-diplomats for the government. They will be encouraged to support the endangered regime values in general terms, along with the specific government policy, probably (i.e. pedagogically demonstrating to the public, how this policy safeguards the regime values). Press loyalty may also prevent external powers from watching the regime in the cards and get access to sensitive information.

Finally, popular cohesion and regime support are salient. Popular reactions to external danger will probably be less calculated than the reasonings referred to above. It is corroborated in experimental psychology that cohesion provides the much needed anxiety reduction in a danger situation through, e.g., the comfort of being with others; also people manifest a need to lean on strong leadership when they are threatened (Stein, 1976, p. 152). Even though extrapolation to the macro level is not unproblematic, this latter finding should explain why popular cohesion is typically channelled into support for the existing regime (unless it has compromised itself, of course). Moreover, danger furthers ethnocentrism and nationalism at the macro level, which in turn promote cohesion and regime support (LeVine and Campbell 1972; Snyder 1993).

Where the Theory does not Apply. In the wake of these arguments supporting the proposition, I should also address its main limits: that the *initial* solidarity among sub-units (i.e. prior to the external pressure) does not exceed a critical threshold (Coser, 1956, p. 93; Otterbein in anthropology[10]), or that the external pressure does not apply evenly (roughly speaking) to the subunits (ibid.; Mintz 1951)[11]. The asserted relationship holds true only if

---

10   According to Otterbein's anthropological studies of warfare, internal cohesion increases as a result of external conflict only when the group possesses a centralized system where the authorities are capable of intervening to create internal cohesion (Stein, 1976, p. 148). Cf. also the insight from social psychology in this regard referred to above.

11   Fritz (1961) summarizes in a survey of psychological research on major disasters that one major condition for unity and solidarity to arise in a group being exposed to it is that *all are affected indiscriminately* so that the danger and suffering become public phenomena that are equally shared. In a longer time perspective, social distinctions may be eliminated or reduced by such an experience.

(a) the group [is] a 'going concern', i.e., there must be a minimal consensus among the constituent individuals that the aggregate is a group, and that its preservation as an entity is worthwhile; (b) there [is] recognition of an outside threat which is thought to menace the group as a whole, not just some part of it (Williams, 1947, p. 58; cf. also Stein, 1976, pp. 144-5).

If the 'critical threshold' (Coser) or the 'minimal consensus' (Williams) were included as a parameter for the proposition here, we would obviously run the risk of making it circular — *unless the threshold be indicated independently from the pressure, we are interested in.* This can be done regarding the present version of the proposition: the threshold is simply given by the existence of a regime and its subunits. By definition, these subunits have not actively laid a distance to the regime prior to the emergence of the external danger challenging the regime. This can be observed *independently* from their subsequent reaction to danger. The theoretical expectation is that they will not be disloyal now but, quite to the contrary, increase their loyalty and become more regime supportive (previously having been only tacitly supportive, perhaps). By contrast, those who *have* laid a distance to the regime in advance are simply not part of it and therefore beyond the scope of the proposition (for instance the Germans and other minorities in Czechoslovakia prior to the Munich crisis 1938, cf. Vital 1971, or Mouritzen 1997b pp. 42-8).

Regarding the second limit, in those cases where the subunits are affected in grossly different ways, the regime will have institutionalized means of rewarding those sub-units that are the least affected (or even positively affected) by the external challenge—what I label *'solidarity reward'* (Mouritzen 1997b ch.1). They are rewarded for not being regime unsolidaric. In other words, the regime is ready to pay for cohesion and, hence, self-control. For instance, the British 'Beveridge Report' during World War II stimulated discussion about the policy of social reform to be pursued after the war. Sir Beveridge gave expression to the widely held belief that the war would be followed by a period of working class radicalism (socialism/communism as an alternative). Therefore, the broad mass of people had better be rewarded for its solidarity with the national war effort (Molin, 1983, p. 326). Part of the explanation for the radical land reform in Finland during and after World War II was the concern that Soviet egalitarian propaganda could appeal to poor people. Hence, they should be rewarded for not falling prey to it (Soikkanen, 1979, p. 107). The Soviet Union rewarded the Ukraine for her solidarity vis à vis the German challenge during World War II by informally making her a junior partner (after Russia) in the Soviet Union, for instance (Subtelny 1988, ch.25).

Reversibility?   As the theory has been formulated, it should be reversible. However, it does not say when and to what extent self-control will wane with subsequently decreasing danger. In particular the popular dimension of self-control may have waned already *before* that time, as a state of readiness or even emergency is probably difficult to retain for a longer time-span[12]. For instance, as reported by Levy (1989a) based on Cotton's study of 5 US wars since 1898,

> If the war drags on...if important national interests are not perceived to be at stake, and if the war effort is not perceived to be unambiguously effective, the war will have detrimental effects on the political leaders involved in initiating the war (p. 312)[13].

Conversely, the governmental-bureaucratic dimension of self-control may last longer than the danger that justified it in the first place, as suitable bureaucratic inertia mechanisms are likely to have emerged in the meantime to support it (Mouritzen, 1988, Part IV).

In other words, it seems in our terminology here that the timing of relaxation after a period of strained regime control may occur differently in different dimensions.

Non-Mobility Revisited

In the thought experiment of states like floating vessels in the sea, any state would have to be alert all the time, since it could expect on short notice to be confronted with one of the most powerful and threatening states in the system. It would have to arrange itself according to a situation of maximum external danger, just to be on the 'safe' side. This would mean, in accordance with the sociological theory presented above, that we could expect a maximum of cohesion and centralization in every unit, in principle. It would be most urgent, evidently, in the small units, given the greater relative dangers they tend to be exposed to.

In international politics characterized by units' mutual non-mobility,

---

12   E.g. Stein (1976, p. 150); on the time factor in general, cf. ibid., pp. 158-9.

13   By contrast, as to the harmonizing effects of World War II on class or regional differences in the Nordic countries, cf. Soikkanen (1979, pp. 131-2). This was true most markedly for Finland with her obvious class differences and the prolonged front experiences during the two wars with the Soviet Union.

however, states will face stable salient environments, as already analysed in chapter 2. These will be of very different natures: some states will be located in dangerous environments, others in favourable ones with no significant security problem, and still others somewhere in-between. In the unfavourably located states we will see cohesion and centralization, following the sociological theory. That means that we should expect little or no independent role to internal factors; the external situation will forbid that luxury. By contrast, in the favourably located states centralization/cohesion will be much lower (at least for this reason)[14]. The leaderships will relax and allow 'democratic luxury' in the formulation of foreign policy; internal factors will exert an influence of their own on foreign policy.

Of course, the picture is not entirely as static as here described. There can be fluctuations in external danger level in all kinds of salient environment, and even if these are stable, they are not eternal. So with era shifts, we may also face shifts in the states' cohesion-centralization and thereby in the independent foreign policy impact of internal factors. Following the theory, however, it is essential to stress that the state leaderships remain in *ultimate control* also as they allow themselves to relax. Relaxation can take place exactly because the leadership is basically in control. That means that it can tighten the ropes again, should the salient environment develop unfavourably.

This is in harmony with the control-relax model as presented initially; non-mobility and thereby the stability of environments for whole eras entails that their essential features are tailored to the kind of parameter function that they are ascribed in this model. These features are *constant* for long periods; hence, they are not fruitfully seen as variables but instead as parameters. In the control-relax model, the sources of external policy are often internal but the state of the environment is assumed to determine their actual influence.

The fact that external factors are also seen as *directly* influencing policy (fig. 6.2) may need a few comments. It is a truism that the environment must be perceived and interpreted by decision-makers in order to have an impact. But as we classify explanatory levels here, it is only the level that carries the *burden* of explanation that we emphasize: the one that can account for most of the variance in policy content. If external conditions are processed through domestic politics and the decision-making apparatus without being exposed to any systematic imprint, then the environment is obviously the causally active factor. This is the significance of the sloping arrow in fig. 6.2. If internally

---

14 Of course there may be a counter-regime that a military dictatorship uses as an excuse for its authoritarian rule.

Fig. 6.2 The control-relax model during 'relax': the external and the permitted internal factors can be added

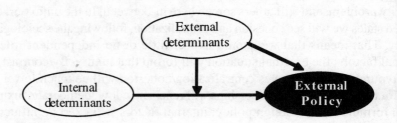

driven policy is allowed simultaneously, it should be obvious that addition between the two sets takes place in turn.

In the information model of fig. 6.1 the sources are external, but internal information processing is assumed to affect the resulting external policy (Goldmann 1976, p. 302). The information model is actually tailored to a system of *mobile* units: the persistently changing environment that each unit experiences makes the environment, also in its basic traits, an obvious variable rather than a parameter. But for a system of non-mobile units like international politics, it is not enough that the information model recognizes external factors as the ultimate variables (source of behaviour). These factors are not ascribed proper 'control' with the workings of internal factors at later stages in the process – and thereby with policy content.

There is one *further* implication flowing from non-mobility and a stable salient environment: its very stability entails that top decision-makers together with bureaucracy and domestic political actors get use to it, both its substance and its SOPs (cf. p. 12). A certain pattern of rhetoric and a bureaucratic code language develop. National stereotypes may be applied to units in the neighbourhood: 'big brother complexes' (at the popular level, notably) or the 'hereditary enemy'. The salient environment, including its challenges and the preferred ways of dealing with them get domestic institutionalization (sedimentation, learning)[15]. In this way, domestic actors can be used by the foreign policy leadership to push in the 'right' direction. With this implication in mind, we can refine the basic control-relax model somewhat.

---

15 Of course, lessons of a more general nature – i.e. improving one's manoeuvering abilities – will be drawn by mobile units. But there will be no learning pertaining to the substance and intricacies of a specific environment as described here.

Control, Relax, Guide

Within the confines of the control-relax interplay, we should now think of three distinct possibilities: 1) the salient environment virtually forbidding the role of internal factors (control); 2) the salient environment leaving ample space for independent roles to internal factors (relax); and 3) the salient environment through the unit leadership 'guiding' the domestic political actors (sedimentation, learning), so as to make them push in the same direction regarding foreign policy as the environment factors themselves (guide).

An example of *control* could be Finland 1944-61 (approx.) In order to safeguard Finnish core values in the wake of the two military defeats against the Soviet Union and the dramatic change in Finland's strategic environment 1944, a posture of adaptive acquiescence towards the Soviet Union was initiated. With strong anti-Soviet feelings residing in the population since the inter-war years and the war experiences, a determined adaptive effort by the President was required (and implemented). President Paasikivi kept a tight grip on all foreign relations, but in particular relations with the eastern neighbour; generally, a centralization of foreign policy decision-making took place (Karvonen, 1984). Censorship in the immediate post-war years and self-censorship were accepted; trials against the 'war responsible' Finnish politicians (enjoing a good deal of popular support) had to be conducted. In other words, the luxury of independent domestic influence on foreign policy could not be afforded; domestic sources of foreign policy were suppressed. The success of the dramatic U-turn in the Finnish posture 1944 in the light of the new environmental strategic situation made this suppression necessary.

According to the *relax* mode of interplay, domestic/democratic influence on external policy is more the rule than the exception. This privilege is not reserved for great powers; weak powers within the confines of NATO, for instance, enjoy a certain leeway for domestic influence. Popular resistance to the modernization of NATO nuclear weapons in the early 1980s was allowed to play a role in the policy of certain member countries; in the case of 'foot-dragging' Denmark, it actually manifested itself in policy outcomes (socalled 'footnotes', e.g., in NATO communiqués).

An example of the *guide* interplay could be found by returning to the Finnish example. After a period of 'good neighbourly relations' with the Soviet Union, the Finnish adaptive posture became gradually internalized in the Finnish political system. In particular in the wake of Finnish-Soviet crises 1958 and 1961, this pattern became clear. Soviet interferences in Finnish politics became less frequent, because they were unnecessary. The requirements of the external situation had *sedimented* at lower levels: all major political parties came to accept the post-1944 foreign policy, and popular opinion increasingly supported the Treaty of Friendship, Cooperation and Mutual Assistance with the Soviet Union (FCMA), according to opinion polls. In this way, lower levels could come to underpin the course chosen for external reasons. Even though their independent influence was questionable, it was at least assured that factors at these levels would not create difficulties for the adaptive course. It was unnecessary to forbid them.

Sedimentation may occur also during 'fair weather' postures. The US being surrounded by two oceans, it is no wonder that democratic/legalistic luxury has persisted in US foreign policy. This is reflected in Congressional influence at the expense of the executive (the President), but one could also emphasize sub-governmental autonomy: '...wherever you go in London to different departments you get the same answer, whereas in Washington each agency will express its own and often competitive view' (Crowe, 1993, p. 182)[16].

Inertia and Foreign Policy Lessons

One thing is guidance in the form of sedimentation/learning. Should this take place one might even imagine that the sediments at various levels continue to affect policy also *after* the end of the era that created them. Top decision-makers as well as bureaucracy repeat behaviour defined as 'successes' or shun behaviour defined as 'failures' (e.g. Steinbruner, 1974; Jervis, 1976; Stenelo, 1981; Levy, 1994). Present behaviour depends not only on present conditions, but also the way incoming information is interpreted in terms of theories inherited from the past. Decision-makers may overlook that evidence supporting their theory may also be consistent with other theories or sheer coincidence (Jervis, ibid). Applying a theory requires historical analogy (Stenelo, 1981; Steinbruner, 1974, pp. 115-16): a current situation is said to be somehow 'similar' to a historical situation (e.g. 'this is like Hitler's march into the Rhineland', as Eden said about Nasser's seizure of the Suez canal zone in 1956). Between the extremes of success and failure, we have precedence thinking both at the top and, even more, in bureaucracy; previous decisions

---

16 Even the US has been exposed to the danger/self control dynamics, however: racial cohesion developed during World War II in spite of Japanese penetration attempts, the seemingly general 'rally around the flag' effect during international crises, and the US decision centralization during the Cuban missile crisis.

or existing routines have a tremendous normative power when 'similar' situations are being faced (SOPs = standard operating procedures)[17]. The underlying reason here may be not only continuity in personnel, but also bureaucratic socialization and education that transmits patterns of beliefs and responses from one generation of bureaucrats to the next.

A particular risk facing the successful regimes is that 'nothing fails like success' (Jervis, 1976, pp. 278-9): one is tempted to use an old, successful remedy the next time one faces a seemingly 'corresponding' situation. Its peculiarities are overlooked. As formulated by Jervis,

> When the aspects of a situation that make it distinctive are not detected, policies that failed previously will be shunned, and policies that succeeded will be applied again even under conditions that are so different that the earlier outcomes tell little about what the results will be if the policies are repeated (1976, p. 234).

Both positive and negative lessons from the past might be seen as a challenge to the environment primacy advocated here; however, we should remember that the environment of the *previous* era is ultimately 'responsible' for these lessons. For instance, as Sweden's symmetric constellation disappeared with the melting down of the Soviet pole, the non-committed foreign policy course ('neutrality') had sedimented at the decision-making level, the bureaucratic level, in domestic politics and in public opinion for more than a century and proved capable of retarding a policy re-orientation significantly (e.g. Sundelius 1994). And neutrality, in turn, was a reflection of Sweden's previous salient environment.

The Role of Internal Factors in Theory-Building

Given the virtue of simplicity for theory-building (cf. chapter 9), we need a relatively simple skeleton to start out from; if postdictions from this basis fail, we should supplement it with relevant factors, if necessary from other levels (or modify/discard the theory, if the deviations form a systematic pattern). In view of the sociological theory and the non-mobility argument, the salient environment has primacy *also* in relation to internal factors. Statistically, it might very well be found that internal factors for most countries' foreign policies most of the time are actually the strongest causes. However,

---

17 On foreign policy inertia in general, cf. Goldmann (1982) or Mouritzen (1988, part IV).

armed with the sociological theory we can be convinced that such a seeming strength is only conditional. The advent of external danger will reduce or eliminate the importance of internal factors. Internal factors' relation to foreign policy cannot be understood independently from the nature of the salient environment, whereas the latter can be understood on its own terms. The implication is that *we cannot build a theoretical skeleton starting out from internal factors; the building must start out from the salient environment and then, if necessary, add internal factors in the light of postdiction failures.* It must start out from the 'foreign sources of foreign policy' – from what foreign policy is all *about.*

As to the 'control' situation – environment factors virtually forbidding the effects of internal factors – there is simply no role to bother about for such factors. Regarding the 'relax' situation with ample space for internal factors, the logic of the theoretical propositions should resemble those in the previous chapter: constellation as parameter for 'if..., then...' propositions. The constellation should be a 'fair weather' one, of course, the initial condition an internal factor, and the dependent variable foreign policy content. Also the 'guide' situation may pave the way for incorporation of internal factors into propositions, but only in so far as inertia/applied lessons are at stake: sedimentation with no future policy effect would be an epi-phenomenon. Inertia can be formulated as a change reducing/ retarding addendum, modifying a basic proposition concerning the (seldom) transformation of a salient environment. Likewise, applied positive/negative foreign policy lessons could be added as modifiers to a more basic proposition. That will be illustrated in the following chapter.

7 Two Illustrations of Interplay

In this chapter I shall provide two illustrations of the interplay between a salient environment theory and domestic politics factors. In both illustrations, the theory deals with bandwagoning in the face of unipolarity: in the former case a unipole with predominantly negative sanctions (alliance theory somewhat refined from chapter 5); in the latter case bandwagoning in the face of a 'pole of attraction' with predominantly positive sanctions (the process of regional EU integration).

In the former illustration, the (refined) theory is combined with an explanatory mechanism about foreign policy lessons learnt from past experience (cf. chapter 6); in the latter, all kinds of domestic political factors are at stake.

It was argued in chapter 5 that balancing/bandwagoning should preferably be understood in a trend perspective, as distinct from the existing literature: bandwagoning – supporting the winner – refers, hence, to the trend-winner, who may be the under-dog in absolute terms. And 'support' may actually mean a less hostile attitude than previously. In this way, balancing/bandwagoning was made a logically exhaustive typology. The theory that was tested asserted that bandwagoning would primarily characterize states subject to a unipolar salient environment; the question whether they are 'small' or not-so-small was argued to be irrelevant, by and large.

Learning within Geopolitical Parameters: Alliance Policy from Helsinki to Warsaw

The integration of bandwagoning theory with the mechanism of foreign policy learning, inter alia, will be illustrated from alliance politics in Europe's Baltic rim from 1988 to the present day (Mouritzen 1998). We include countries that 1) border Russia and 2) are seriously discussed as future NATO-members: Finland, Estonia, Latvia, Lithuania and Poland (the two latter bordering the Russian Kaliningrad enclave). From a superficial glance these states might seem to have similar salient environments. At least at the outset of the period, they all (more or less) belonged to the sphere of the Soviet unipole; that is, the Soviet Union possessed by far the most significant (negative) sanctions of relevance for these countries[1]. Finland and Poland, as part of the process, definitely slipped out of the Russian orbit with the dissolution of the Soviet Union.

Since the Cold War the Soviet Union/Russia was obviously the power loser and the US/the West consequently the power winner. Bench marks here were Soviet troop withdrawals from Eastern Europe from 1988, the fall of the Berlin Wall and the East European revolutions 1989 and, first and foremost, the dissolution of the Soviet Union 1991. The 'losses' of the Baltic countries and the Ukraine, in particular, were geo-political blows in relation to the West. To this should be added the gradual reduction in Russian military strength since then, due not least to general demoralisation in the armed forces.

How have the rim states reacted to this revision of the balance of power in their salient environment? For *Finland,* we saw in chapter 5 that its major re-orientation in the post-war period (declaring a wish for EU membership, recognition of the Baltic countries, distance to the FCMA Treaty) occured in September 1991, as the Soviet Union and its ideology disintegrated. It is noteworthy that the revolutions in East and Central Europe 1989-90 made little or no impression on Finnish policy; the crucial factor was the power structure in Finland's immediate neighbourhood that was not transformed until September 1991. Finland bandwagoned towards and eventually into the EU, but it stopped there. Even if all options were explicitly held open, Finland did not declare any specific aspiration to join NATO. Also in order not to provoke Russia, Finland was somewhat more cautious in military cooperation with the Baltic countries than were Sweden and Denmark.

Estonia, Latvia, and Lithuania went through strikingly parallel developments in their declaratory policies. During their rather symbolic independencies prior to international recognition in September 1991, they aimed for 'neutrality' and a demilitarized status. The idea of a nuclear-free zone in the Baltic Sea area that had been debated in various forms in the Nordic countries was also supported. These declarations were attempts to signal a difference from the Soviet Union and were probably also thought to be instrumental in would-be negotiations concerning Soviet troop withdrawals. During the interim period between international recognitions and the Russian troop withdrawals (August 1993 from Lithuania, August 1994 from Estonia and Latvia), aspirations were

---

1   Finland's (high politics) dependence on the Soviet Union was due to her being in an asymmetrical constellation in the East-West bipolarity (cf. chapter 5) or, to use an alternative formulation, *weak* Moscow unipolarity in Helsinki. This latter formulation will be used in the present chapter.

heightened. Whereas 'neutrality' had previously provided a symbolic link to the inter-war republics, the traumatic outcomes of these neutrality policies, i.a., made 'neutrality' an impossible option in the formulation of proper security policies. Among various Western international organizations, also NATO membership was openly mentioned as a possibility. Apart from getting the former Soviet troops out of the countries, the main Baltic priority in this period was to avoid being seen as Russian 'near abroad', both by Russia and the West. It was vital not to be lumped together in any contexts with the CIS countries. After the troop withdrawals from the three countries, the EU and NATO membership strivings became more substantial (e.g. Europe agreements in June 1995, active participation in NATO's PfP). Lithuania even applied officially for NATO membership in January 1994.

Even though internal developments in *Poland* were to a large extent an ice-breaker in relation to Soviet domination of Eastern Europe, the new Polish democratic regime adapted to a large extent its foreign policy (alliance) orientation to trends in the Soviet power position. Even though the attitude seemed to be 'leave every Eastern institution; join every Western one', Poland was anxious not to rock the boat too much: EC membership was high on the agenda in contrast to NATO membership that would have provoked the Soviet Union. Instead, the role of the CSCE for the future European security order was emphasized. With the revolution of Poland's salient environment through the proliferation of neighbours 1990-91, implying inter alia that Poland no longer bordered mainland Russia, NATO membership officially entered the agenda and eventually became priority no.1. Poland was welcomed into NATO at the NATO Madrid summit of 1997.

The general pattern seems to be that the weaker the Soviet Union/Russia and thereby also the less threatening, the more the rim states turned away from it, paradoxically as it may sound at first sight. Thereby, they weakened its position further. In short, they (trend-) bandwagoned as defined in chapter 5.

How Much Bandwagoning?

The universal trend in the sphere of a unipole – and a little bit beyond – is bandwagoning. However, powers do it to various extents. Some of them move from being part of the unipole to an opposing alliance (or at least aspire to join it), others move just a little bit: out of the unipole sphere, but not enough to enter an opposing alliance, or modestly within an opposing alliance (the weak front-line state). Whereas the Finnish re-orientation was a watershed measured with the yardstick of Finnish post-war policy, it was modest in comparison with those of the four other countries.

Turning to a *status* instead of a trend perspective, the outcome so far is NATO membership for Poland, for others strong willingness to attain such (the Baltic countries), and for Finland an unprecedented 'openness to all options' – including NATO membership. These provisional outcomes can be expressed in terms of the states' handling of the 'abandonment/entrapment' dilemma as presented by Snyder (1984). Two evils must somehow be mutually rated by any alliance candidate: what is feared the most, being left alone with the perceived danger (abandonment), or being drawn into war that could otherwise have been avoided (entrapment)? As we shall see below, none of the five countries seem to experience much of a dilemma. For Finland, whereas entrapment is an evil, abandonment is actually seen as a good thing. In other words, there is no dilemma at stake under the prevailing circumstances. The four other countries do not experience a dilemma, either, but for almost the opposite reason. Abandonment is an evil, but entrapment is an *unavoidable* evil. In other words, all energy should be mobilized to avoid abandonment. Again, there is no dilemma at stake, since the choice is so self-evident.

Why is it that Finland comes out so differently from the other four countries in making the abandonment/entrapment priority? Or to put it differently: why is it that Finland bandwagons so relatively little and the other four so much? The reasons are twofold, but intertwined. They will here be formulated in general terms:

1)   *A status quo oriented vs. a revisionist unipole.* In relation to a basically status quo oriented (conservative) unipole, it makes sense to safeguard a reasonable liquidity of goodwill at the pole, so that it remains satisfied. There is really something to lose by counter-balancing: the 'hawks' (or even reckless forces) in the domestic politics of the unipole might gain influence and perhaps even come to power. Therefore only cautious bandwagoning will take place, and hardly all the way into an opposing alliance. By contrast, goodwill is wasted in relation to a revisionist (or even reckless) unipole. Its aggression bound to come sooner or later will be encouraged by a friendly attitude. Alliance with the opposing pole is the only sensible option, if at all available. So should an opportunity arise, the unit will bandwagon as quickly as possible; it has nothing to lose.

One may ask why this factor has affected Finland differently from the four other countries? After all, the five countries were (are) dealing with the same unipole. Still, *differential impact* was clearly possible. Irrespective of decision-makers and their perceptions in each rim-state (cf. below), Finland and to some extent Poland faced a Russia that was different from that facing the Balts. Should Russian revisionism occur, the Baltic countries could be expected as its first targets, since they had recently been Soviet republics. Poland gradually became unlikely as target of would-be Russian/Soviet revisionism, although its status as former Warsaw Pact member and its geopolitical in-between position could not be ignored. Finland with its geopolitically remote location was safer, and any revisionism in that direction would have to be based on far-fetched pre-World War I inspiration[2]. In other words, one and the same unipole revisionism may apply differently to different countries. In this sense, even salient environments that are similar at a high level of abstraction turn out, on closer inspection, to be somewhat different. And in this case, that difference has significant implications for behaviour.

2)   *The foreign policy lessons.* The differential impact argument is based, inter alia, on the countries' different historical positions in relation to the unipole. These have also entailed that forceful, but contradictory, foreign policy *lessons* have sedimented in the five countries. Finland learned from the inter-war years and World War II that alliances and alliance speculations are dangerous; if need be, Finland can manage on her own militarily. The post-war lesson was that Finland could manage on her own politically as well; it was actually possible to do business with a status quo oriented Eastern neighbour. So the two heritages amounted to one and the same lesson: 'do it yourself'; being virtually abandoned is actually a good thing (the lesson had also sedimented at the popular level: only 21% pro NATO membership 1996). The four other countries have made the opposite experience. Being dominated by the Soviet Union (Poland) or subject to occupation (the Baltic countries) after World War II have entailed perceptions of this unipole as being by nature aggressive and dominating, the 'empire of evil', be its name the 'Soviet Union' or 'Russia'. The current Russia is and will be revisionist, even if it may manage to conceal this to the West. Whereas entrapment will happen in any case when bordering such a power, abandonment is an evil that should be avoided almost at any price. With this perception, quick bandwagoning to the opposite camp is the sensible strategy, if and when the opportunity presents itself. As the experiences of 1939-40 showed, the Baltic countries could not stand on their own militarily, and Poland was caught between two enemies. NATO's and the EU's assets are not *only* their hard and soft deterrence vis à vis a revisionist

---

2   Finland was a Tsarist Grand-Duchy prior to 1917.

Russia, but also – notably for Poland – their dependency spreading and 'Einbindung' of Germany (1939!).

Summing up, whereas it was natural for these countries to shun abandonment almost at any price (entrapment being unavoidable), for Finland abandonment was a good thing and entrapment an evil that could be avoided. So the choices were easy for all five, albeit they were made differently; none of them experienced a dilemma. We should remember, however, that the basic law of (trend) bandwagoning applied to all of them; the difference was that Poland and the Baltic countries bandwagoned much more than Finland.

Theory of alliance policy should be formulated relative to the polarity prevailing in states' salient environment, not their size; subject to unipolarity as in the cases of this chapter, states will bandwagon in accordance with the power trend prevailing, be they 'small' or not so small. This is the basic law. To which *degree* will depend not only on further geopolitical features, but also on their past salient environment and past policy successes/failures.

The House was merely Overheated

This was a combination of a theory anchored at the salient environment level with a mechanism pertaining to a set of internal factors (foreign policy lessons). The basic theory was that of bandwagoning. Presupposing unipolarity in the unit's salient environment (the parameter), the more the balance of power shifts in this environment to the advantage of the unipole (the independent variable), the more the unit will support this unipole (the dependent variable) – and vice versa. This is the basic law; together with the reasonings for it, it constitutes a theory. It is illustrated by the sloping arrow in fig. 6.2: it goes directly from the external power trend to a trend in its behaviour. The house is on fire in Wolfer's terminology; all units in the unipole sphere are expected to do likewise, i.e. rush towards the entrance.

However, the situation was not that simple; there was more to it than that prescribed by the basic theory. On the one hand, there were further geopolitical factors (differential impact). On the other hand, the five nation-states were all in favourable external situations compared to previous times, and the pendulum was therefore on 'relax' in terms of the 'control-relax' conception. Internal factors were *allowed* an influence on alliance policy. The most forceful domestic factor was that of foreign policy lessons inherited from the previous era. The lesson learnt in Finland was widely different from those that had sedimented in the four other countries. In these four, the Russia hatred and

Russia fear sedimenting in the populations for decades had now direct access to top decision-makers (some of them probably sharing these feelings). In Finland, popular NATO reluctance probably reinforced decision-makers' own reluctance. The lessons *added* to the basic pattern of bandwagoning that all five exhibited; the result was that Finland just bandwaggoned a little bit, whereas the remaining four bandwagoned extensively. To return to Wolfer's terminology: the house was not on fire; it was merely overheated. Hence, the external compulsion was not strong enough to make everyone act alike; one hurried out of the door, three were looking eagerly for it, whereas one just opened a window. So in spite of a certain common compulsion, individual predispositions were allowed to play a significant role as well.

European Integration and National Bandwagoning 1989-94: Facing a Pole of Attraction

Let us turn to yet another illustration of the primacy of salient environment at the expense of various sets of domestic factors, as prescribed by the control-relax model. Mouritzen, Wæver, and Wiberg (1996) drew a European *'value map'*, elucidating which national actors were gaining (the 'dominant' ones), which were losing (those in 'adaptive acquiescence'), which were both simultaneously (the 'balanced' ones)[3], and which were neither (the 'quiescent' ones), from their various post-1989 challenges. Such a map, evidently, invites the question of causality: which were the driving forces being responsible for the various value statuses? The overall European polarity shift – from regional bipolarity to regional EU unipolarity, cf. chapter 4 in the present book – cannot in itself account for the heterogeneity in value statuses. That brought us to the notion of 'constellation' and the core question: how can we theoretically link constellation type and value status (= 'mode of adaptation')?

The model with this ambition that will be formulated here is an empirical idealtype that summarizes a welter of empirical detail (cf. also Mouritzen 1996a). But it also adds abstract theoretical principles, precisely in order to achieve the simplification that is necessary for the purpose of presenting a relatively coherent value picture of Europe.

The model is formulated as a *general* one regarding the adaptation of non-essential powers during unipolar regional integration. The non-essential

---

3   This balanced value status should not be confused, of course, with 'balancing' in the balancing/bandwagoning typology in alliance theory.

powers are those that do not *constitute* the power structure at stake – i.e. all actors except for Germany and France, whose mutual axis is a prerequisite for the current structure. The non-essential powers are not in a position to transform the European power structure, but they can relate/adapt to it in various ways.

It was decided to distinguish between three constellations during European unipolar integration (cf. chapter 4): EC/EU insiders, would-be insiders and outsiders. The model then asserts that constellation is systematically related to a certain value status – mode of adaptation – for national actors located in them. The model, as depicted in figure 7.1, indicates what kind of restrictions that the unipolar integration structure confers upon nation-states in each constellation and, by consequence, what room there is for alternative sources of nation-state behaviour. Hence, in accordance with the control-relax principle the model assumes that the polarity restrictions have primacy in relation to other conceivable restrictions on decision-makers: they may *permit* the workings of the latter and thereby leave space for them in a particular constellation or situation. To put it differently, the *permissive* cause (polarity restriction) may sometimes allow other factors to function as the *efficient* or immediate cause. The underlying justification for this alleged primacy is that a unipole has no competitors on its own level (cf. further below); secondly, the question of unipole membership is such an all-encompassing matter for

Fig. 7.1 National adaptation to (regional) unipolar integration: a general model

	Polarity restrictions on behaviour	Leeway for alternative restrictions	Mode of Adaptation
Outsiders	Broader dependency (modest)	Plenty, all kinds	Weak adaptive acquiescence or quiescent mode, notably
Would-be insiders	1) Rules and norms of the pole, as interpreted by the pole; appeasement of potential 'vetoers' 2) Goodwill Competition 3) Broader Dependency (strong)	None	Adaptive acquiescence or identification
Insiders	Rules and norms of the pole, but subject to own influence and a wide range of interpretations	Plenty, domestic including historical restrictions, notably	Balanced mode (including wide range of specific behaviour)

a national actor (including both traditional high and low politics) that it is likely to take precedence over any rivalling concerns. Turning to the far right column, the model indicates what mode of adaptation that will occur – with more precision for some constellations than for others, though.

Starting with the *would-be insiders,* they feel that they must abide by the rules and norms of the pole wherever relevant – as these are interpreted by the pole or its prime members, one should stress. As such interpretations are not always made explicit, they will have to be anticipated ('anticipated reaction'). This type of behaviour can be expected for the simple reason that the would-be insiders wish to appear as natural future insiders – in case as 'good Europeans'. Specifically, it is crucial that those members that can be feared, potentially, to veto their entrance (or at any rate postpone it) are appeased – or are not offered arguments, at least, that can be used as pretexts for their opposition to membership. These various goodwill considerations should be supplemented by a competitive mechanism: it could be feared that *other* would-be insiders might manage to get first in the queue and, hence, delay one's own membership for an indefinite time period. Such fear will probably lead to a goodwill competition that may induce goodwill behaviour far beyond what the insiders have expected. Bandwagoning is obviously at stake: the stronger and more credible the pole (a 'pole of attraction' with mostly positive sanctions), the more it will be appeased. This tendency will be self-reinforcing, because everybody else apparently does likewise and jumps on the bandwagon.

In addition to the above mechanisms that are closely related to the question of membership, there will also be *broader* patterns of dependency – economically, regarding identity, or generally in the geographic neighbourhood of the pole that the would-be insider is normally situated in. The salient environment of the would-be insider is markedly *unipolar;* there is no alternative pole within reach that could provide beneficial playing off opportunities. This pattern of dependency is costly to break.

For instance, even though Latin-American countries do not aspire to become members of the 'United States of America', they are nonetheless subject to varying degrees of dependency on the US in this broader sense. As with the membership considerations, the dependency pattern will be a parameter not only for direct relations with the pole – or its members – but also for relations with third parties in the world around. The pole's behaviour vis à vis third countries will typically be imitated or approximated.

In view of these two powerful categories of restrictions on behaviour, there is no space for the influence of rivalling explanatory factors, such as domestic ones or other external ones. The would-be insider's behaviour should be conceptualized relative to its prevailing regime values (cf. chapter 4). If they happen to coincide completely with those of the pole, we face sheer identification: one does not 'adapt' to a value that one basically shares. If, however, there are differences, then we are dealing with adaptive acquiescence: the regime reluctantly accepts infringements on one or more of its values in order to preserve more basic values. The latter possibility is likely to be the typical one; after all, any political actor will normally appreciate its own autonomy, even if all other values should coincide with those of its salient environment. The very *degree* of adaptive acquiescence will be dependent on the degree of asymmetry in the pattern of dependency at stake. For instance, a would-be insider that is likely to become a future net receiver from EU budgets is probably involved in more pronounced adaptive acquiescence than one that is likely to become a net contributor.

Given the sheer number of would-be insiders in the post-1989 era – realistically aspiring for membership either in a short-term or mid-term perspective – one can safely expect a proliferation of adaptive acquiescence compared to the bipolar period. During the latter epoch, this generally infrequent mode of adaptation (Mouritzen 1988, pp. 373-76) was represented in Europe by the Finland, solely, being subject to weak unipolar conditions in her salient environment. But as the overall European power structure has turned unipolar, a whole belt of national actors have adopted this mode of adaptation from the early 1990s.

Turning to the *outsiders,* the polarity structure exerts considerably less influence on their behaviour. As membership is not on the agenda, they are liberated from the kind of specific goodwill considerations that the would-be insiders are subject to. Still, the broader unipolar dependency is likely to play a role. But it will probably be a minor one than described for the previous constellation, due to the outsiders' relative geographical remoteness from the pole. Taken together, this means that 'relax' rather than 'control' will prevail; there is plenty of leeway for alternative sources of behaviour as efficient causes, be they domestic or external ones. For instance, the proliferation of new states and disputed borders as in post-Cold War Europe has created new *local* polarities that to some extent blur the effects of the prevailing regional unipolarity.

With these various sources of behaviour, several behavioural types will be represented within the outsider constellation. One can imagine a quiescent mode of adaptation (the voluntary outsider Switzerland) or weak adaptive acquiescence (the aspiring outsider Romania) as the most typical modes[4]. A dominant mode of adaptation would be excluded by definition, given the unipolar nature of the overall power structure; but a locally defiant posture such as that of Yugoslavia during the Ex-Yugoslav civil war is a possibility.

Jumping to the *insiders,* they resemble the outsiders in that they enjoy a reasonable action space – even though for widely different reasons[5]. They are subject to the rules and norms of the pole in a variety of issue-areas; but in contrast to the would-be insiders, they exert an influence on the construction of these rules and norms as well as on their specific interpretation. This leaves plenty of room for the influence of domestic factors (e.g., Moravscick 1991; Garrett 1992, pp. 541, 548; Haahr 1993) on the insider decision-makers (or through transnational channels, one could add), but also for the role of ideology and historical factors such as foreign policy tradition or traumatic events in the past. This variety of behavioural sources means that we can hardly generalize much about the *specific* behaviour at stake. But by way of exclusion, we can argue that a *balanced* mode of adaptation will prevail: historically unprecedented interdependence among the insiders will prevent a quiescent or a dominant mode[6], and domestic opinion and interest groups will rule out adaptive acquiescence. The EU internal market is actually a paradigm example of a hyper-balanced mode for its participants: through the voting rules they all get an unprecedented influence on the designing of standards and regulations that shall prevail throughout the Community; conversely, they have to live with decisions deeply affecting their societal structures that are not always to their liking.

Within the broad category of a balanced mode of adaptation, however, we may find integration enthusiasts as well as integration skeptics. When accounting for integration attitude, historical experience will play a decisive role. Reducing the priority of autonomy is easiest, evidently, in cases where nationalism or the state apparatus has compromised itself seriously in the past (cf. the periods of dictatorship in this century in Germany, Spain, Portugal,

---

4   In the more elaborate terminology of Wiberg (1996), we should remember that traits of adaptive acquiescence were found among the aspiring outsiders – those who *after all* nourish some wishful thinking about future membership – whereas they were absent among voluntary outsiders and resigned outsiders.

5   As argued by Mouritzen (1996b), even insiders can meaningfully be said to adapt to the pole (pp. 24-5).

6   We should remember here that the model does not apply to the *essential* powers, in case Germany and France. Judged from evidence on the SEA decision (Garrett 1992), they are able to engage in a dominant mode of adaptation, if they can agree mutually.

Italy, or Greece). The shift of loyalty to the 'United States of Europe' will be comparatively easier. Another explanatory factor in this regard is the regime's self-control, e.g. whether it comprises a nationally homogeneous population (Denmark) or not (Belgium). If significant ethnic groups feel alienated, or not very loyal, vis à vis the regime, resistance to reducing or abandoning its autonomy will be low or non-existent.

As should appear from this section, the mode typology as well as the constellation typology should be fruitful from the viewpoint of theory-building, in the sense that they can be systematically related to each other: constellation makes an obvious difference to value status and, thereby, mode of adaptation.

Comparisons: Intra-Constellation and Cross-Constellation

The model can facilitate comparison by putting cases of European national actors into mutual perspective. As to *intra-constellation comparison*, the Danish and Dutch insiders – while both representing a balanced mode of adaptation – express rather different degrees of balancing. Both were pushed by the German unification into more positive (foreign policy) integration attitudes than previously by virtue of advocating an 'Einbindung' as the adequate counter-strategy. But the revisions took place at different levels: Denmark abandoned its previous foot-dragging attitudes, whereas the Netherlands transformed its official federalist position 'from sounds to things'. However, both were corrected and pushed back to their original positions, essentially: the Dutch on a 'black Monday' in October 1991 by their EC partners, the Danish decision-makers on 2 June 1992 by the referendum electorate.

But what can account for the level difference regarding integration enthusiasm between these two insiders? The traditions of maritime commercialism, anti-continentalism, neutralist abstentionism (replaced by atlanticism after World War II) and international idealism are common, by and large. So are non-compromised state apparatuses and relatively homogeneous populations (the Danes, in particular). Two factors with deep historical roots are probably essential for an explanation. Firstly, Denmark saw a serious alternative to EC integration in the Nordic option, especially during the first post-war decades; Benelux co-operation was far from being a Dutch equivalent to this. Secondly, Denmark and the Netherlands had (and have) different ambitions regarding the regime value of offensive power/influence. The Netherlands, with its not-so-distant colonial past and status as an EC founding father, would never be content with the 'small state' influence level that Danish decision-makers find satisfactory, being used to it since 1870, roughly speaking, and being tied by the popular preference for autonomy over influence, cf. Mouritzen 1996a (and the popular belief that 'we Danes' don't have influence anyway, Wæver 1995). Now, the major threat to Dutch influence ambitions is too close German-French cooperation. Close great power cooperation reduces the market value of the assets of non-essential powers; their playing-off opportunities disappear and thereby most of their influence (Rothstein 1968, p. 192; Goldmann 1979b, Mouritzen 1988, p. 238). A major theme in Dutch strategy and rhetoric therefore consists in warnings against a would-be great power directorate, whatever its nature. EC/EU supranationality, including a strong Commission, is seen as a *means* to avoid such great power domination, but in no way a guarantee against it. The Netherlands therefore seeks to pre-empt a development in this direction, chiefly by strengthening EC/EU integration. The Danes with their different influence priority/beliefs do not fear such a development to the same extent, as they (believe to) have very little to lose, anyway, in terms of offensive power.

Whereas the model predicts heterogeneity as the normal situation among insiders and thereby makes plenty of room for the Danish/Dutch heterogeneity, it is silent on the *specific* explanations that can account for the Danish/Dutch mutual difference. These are exogenous to the model, of course.

Comparing the then would-be insiders of Finland and Poland, it is striking how equal their modes and strategies are, given the tremendous differences in historical background and level of economic development among them, and given the different phases that they had reached at the time in their EU approachments. For instance, the EU penchant for all-European stability has been anticipated by Poland through her aspiration to become a 'regional stabilizer' vis à vis ex-Soviet territories, not least. This resembles the Finnish aspiration to assist/stabilize Estonia and the North-Western parts of Russia. This is not really a Finnish concession, being used to a 'friendly' course Eastward (though previously with other means). But Poland, by contrast, anticipates the wishes of the EU unipole and adopts this 'Finnish approach', in spite of its anti-Russian preferences[7]. Moreover, the EU has favoured Visegrad co-operation and Poland has reluctantly anticipated this. As with Nordic co-operation, there have been attempts to use Visegrad as a platform of negotiation vis à vis the EC/EU (actually encouraged by the EU itself).

---

7   As demonstrated by Kostecki & Wiberg (1996), this approach is still in its infancy, and there are still oscillations in Polish/Russian relations that can jeopardize this role.

But on both platforms, goodwill competition among national actors vis à vis the EU has proven stronger than concern for the common platform.

This comparison should illuminate the extraordinary importance of constellation and the unimportance of various nation-state attributes/traditions for would-be insiders. Regimes with extremely heterogeneous attributes and histories have been structurally induced to follow quite similar policies.

Lithuania and the Ukraine have not only their outsider status in common, but also their recent past as ex-Soviet republics. Still, we face not only a heterogeneity of specific policies – as with the insiders – but even a heterogeneity of modes: quiescence for Lithuania and a seemingly inconsistent blend of quiescence and adaptive acquiescence in various directions for the Ukraine. The main explanation for this difference seems to be that the Lithuanian regime has established a clear set of identity values (ethno-nationalism probably being the strongest), whereas its Ukrainian counterpart has not. The existence of the Ukrainian regime is not, like the Lithuanian, the fruit of a long-lasting conscious struggle against the Moscow authorities and it has not the relatively long Lithuanian period of inter-war independence as a source of identity. Moreover, divisions along territorial lines prevail (the territorial size difference is crucial at this point, of course), together with institutional malfunctioning. So it is not surprising that a West-direction competes with an East-direction of adaptive acquiescence, even to the point of mutual inconsistency and confusion.

Comparing these three intra-constellation comparisons, it is striking how easily heterogeneous behaviour comes to characterize insiders and – even more – the outsiders. *Even* though they shared constellation as well as four common traditions and non-compromised state apparatuses (Denmark/the Netherlands) or constellation and ex-Soviet republic status (Lithuania/the Ukraine), the modes were different for the outsiders and the specific behaviour in essential respects for the insiders. In other words: relatively little is enough in these constellations to produce heterogeneous behaviour. The opposite is the case for the would-be insiders: *enormous differences in historical background and economic development are insufficient to produce significant behavioural differences. They are superseded by the restrictions of constellation.*

Turning to *cross-constellation comparison,* one should compare national actors in different constellations facing one and the same challenge. An example could be a comparison of Danish behaviour vis à vis the Maastricht Treaty with the corresponding Swedish behaviour. Whereas Sweden as a would-be insider had to behave like a 'Musterknabe', the Danish insider could afford to be the 'naughty boy' in the European integration class and demand special conditions for itself. A bit paradoxically perhaps, the luxury of integration reluctance can only be enjoyed by those already integrated as insiders. As a corollary of this, the Swedish decision-makers could not afford to express the slightest support for the Danish special arrangement – even though it was in perfect harmony with traditional Swedish neutrality and would have pleased its electorate and thereby increased the prospects of a favourable referendum outcome. Adaptive acquiescence vis à vis the EU at the time made comments on the Danish arrangement extremely sensitive.

As a would-be insider, the parameters of the unipolar power structure were stronger for Sweden than conceivable domestic factors or historical experience (the neutrality tradition). The action space was extremely narrow, hence. One might object here that the fact that Sweden did hold a membership referendum bears witness that domestic factors *were* allowed to exert an influence, to say the least. This is an exception from the model, of course. Theoretically, popular influence on foreign affairs should be at a low ebb during adaptive acquiescence (Mouritzen 1988, pp. 291-2, 322-4). But the point is that in the Swedish case, a referendum would have been unavoidable regarding the constitutional revisions that are necessary for membership – meaning in practice a EU referendum. Moreover, the Swedish popular resistance to the EU that emerged was hardly foreseen by the regime at the time, when the referendum was announced (the polls still being favourable)[8]. At any rate, consistently negative opinion polls in Sweden tended to *improve* the Swedish position in the EU membership negotiations and reduce/eliminate its degree of adaptive acquiescence, as the referendum came into view. The referendum factor seems to have blurred the effects of constellation for Sweden during the second half of 1993 and 1994. However, the primacy of constellation was evident from 1990 through 1991, 1992 and the first part of 1993.

The House Overheated Again

Regarding the would-be insiders, the theory established above is in essence a theory of bandwagoning during unipolarity, just like the one applied to the Baltic rim states in the Soviet/Russian orbit. Only this time, we are dealing

---

8   In Finland a referendum could, theoretically, have been avoided. President Koivisto is reported to have expressed his reluctance towards the idea of a popular EC referendum. However, the fact that other Nordic countries held or have held referendums over roughly the same issue in the past (diffusion!), surely made it difficult to avoid.

with a membership pole and a 'pole of attraction' with mostly positive sanctions.

The theory being anchored at the salient environment level (polarity restrictions as the permissive cause), it should be illustrated how domestic factors including culture, tradition, etc. and various external factors interplay with the theoretically significant external ones. Whereas they are permitted significant roles in the insider and outsider constellations, they are suppressed for the would-be insiders. Thereby, so different nation-states as Poland and Finland (or Sweden for that matter) came to adapt almost identically to the pole. In Wolfer's terminology, the external compulsion was strong. Only the popular EU reluctance in the Swedish case had a marginal influence during 1993 and 1994, as it strengthened the Swedish posture vis à vis the EU somewhat. The house of the would-be insiders was grossly overheated, whereas the insider and outsider houses had more comfortable temperatures.

8 The Role of International Organizations

IGOs: The Control-Relax Mechanism Reapplied

There are other types of actors in international politics than nation-states. Even though a state-centric conception of international politics is being presented in this book, it is important to single out the relationship between states and non-state actors, be it IGOs (international governmental organizations), INGOs (international non-governmental organizations), multinational corporations, or other types of entities. It is essential to identify a pre-theoretical mechanism characterizing the relationship between states and non-states. This mechanism is that of control-relax which was applied throughout chapters 6 and 7 regarding the role of internal factors in foreign policy. It is seen here as relevant in relation to all those types of non-state actors mentioned above; however, I shall apply it only to the relationship between states and IGOs and states and the EU[1].

IGOs have been consciously designed by national governments in order to solve common problems that they cannot solve satisfactorily on their own – be it the regulation of war, trade, or transport or problems pertaining to development, the environment, human rights, etc. IGOs may be of a regional or universal scope (e.g. the 'Organization of African Unity' vs. the United Nations); that distinction is unimportant here. The sheer number of IGOs has grown exponentially during the 20th century, notably after World War II; that is why certain IR schools have ascribed them an increasing importance in international politics, perhaps even rivalling that of nation-states.

As will be argued here, IGOs can be seen as the twining plants of international co-operation: firstly they are weak (cannot keep upright without support), secondly they are beautiful (supposed to serve beautiful purposes) and thirdly they are virtually impossible to get rid of. IGO weakness is most pronounced in high politics. But how can these weak creatures be so difficult to get rid of? Because the most powerful actors in international politics – nation-states – wish IGOs to survive, even if they should appear redundant

---

1   The EU is dealt with separately, because it is such a special kind of entity, surrounded by debates that should be related to. However, the EC/EU will also be used in some illustrations before that, since it shares several inter-governmental qualities with IGOs.

or inefficient in relation to their official purposes. The reason is that IGOs serve certain national vested interests (i.e. behind the facade), including beneficial unintended consequences flowing from their sheer existence. Just as beautiful twining plants can serve to hide ugly walls, for instance. On the one hand, nation-states do not allow IGOs to function too well and become too influential – especially not in high politics. On the other hand, they do not allow them to disappear.

The present chapter is structured around this apparent paradox. A section illustrates the national vested interests that IGOs dominated by high politics can serve – as arenas of nation-state co-operation and conflict and with negligible actorhood of their own. The first (and major) section inquires into the reasons for this IGO lack of actorhood in high politics.

It is actually part of conventional wisdom that 'security' and strong IGOs do not go very well together. This is based on considerable historical/comparative evidence. Even alliances that existed for several decades – e.g. the Triple Entente or the Triple Alliance before World War I – did not become IGOs in the first place. This century – particularly after World War II – has seen several 'security' IGOs, NATO being the prime example. This organization possesses its own bureaucratic structures, military as well as civilian ones. But in its major aspects, it is still a *weak* IGO: member-countries keep a solid grip on its bureaucratic structures and safeguard, by requiring unanimity in the NATO decision-making organs, that decisions are made by consensus. In theory at least, no member-state runs the risk of being forced into measures not to its liking. Turning to collective security, IGOs were created in the form of the League of Nations, the United Nations and the Organization of American States. But the great powers have always kept control through veto-power. No standing military forces have been established (although presently being discussed in the UN). Socalled 'peace-keeping forces' established on an ad-hoc basis with strictly limited mandates have been set in at various trouble-spots. So in spite of the historical trend, 'security' lags significantly behind other areas regarding the role and influence of IGOs; think of, for instance, big and influential UN IGOs like the WHO (medicine) or UNESCO (education, science, culture).

I shall seek to reconstruct here the intermediary reasoning connecting 'security' and weak IGOs in a more explicit way than is usually done (in the form of a general model). Also its underlying assumptions will be highlighted, as well as some empirical evidence. In this way, I shall argue that the conventional wisdom is actually wisdom, although it needs some clarification and elaboration.

The Control-Relax Model for IGOs: its Justification

In chapter 6, the control-relax mechanism pertained to the interplay between salient environment and internal factors in foreign policy explanation. The justification was the sociological theory saying that external danger entails internal cohesion-centralization. This was applied diachronically (over time) for one unit's foreign policy: increasing external danger entails increasing cohesion-centralization. However, one can also apply it synchronically by comparing issue-areas of policy at a given point in time. If more danger to the unit's core values are at stake within one area rather than another, then the unit will centralize and mobilize more cohesion within that area. Democracy will suffer accordingly. That is typically so in foreign policy as distinct from domestic politics, to use the most aggregate categories[2]. The application used here is also synchronic: in some issue-areas governments will hold a tight grip ('control') not only on their own domestic civil services and agencies, but also on the IGOs that they are members of. This in turn pertains to the IGO Council of Ministers and committees of national civil servants at various levels, as well as to the IGO's own bureaucracy consisting of socalled 'international civil servants' (their own compatriots in particular, of course). Even if such a grip is against the staff rules of international civil services, it nonetheless plays a role informally and discreetely. In other issue-areas, however, governments relax their grips in all of these respects.

The model presupposes that IGO influence relative to their member-states varies significantly between issue-areas. The model sets out to explain this variation. There can be different balances of influence within one and the same IGO, if it covers several areas. Also, the balance of influence between IGOs and their member-states is a question of degree, obviously. At the most modest level, the IGO is an *arena* for member-states' cooperation and conflict, solely (e.g. James, 1976, p. 76). Nation-state representatives strive as modern gladiators to come out on top in the diplomatic contest which finds verbal and voting expression in its debating chamber. The IGO serves as a communication facilitator between member-state representatives. At more advanced levels, the IGO's bureaucracy/civil service (its General-Secretary and his/her staff, payed from the IGO budget) acquires *actor* properties (e.g. Cox, 1969), enabling it to exert significant influence of its own on member-countries or other actors (mediate between member-countries, for instance).

---

2   On the 'incompatibility hypothesis' between democracy and foreign policy, cf. Goldmann et.al. (1986).

These actor properties include certain organizational interests (survival and influence-capability/autonomy; cf. Mouritzen, 1990, pp. 12-14) and, hopefully, the values described in the IGO charter – be it global health, security, or whatever. As distinct from member-country representatives (including 'permanent representatives' residing at the IGO Headquarter), the IGO civil service carries most of the IGO identity (Claude, 1964, p. 174). The civil service personifies the IGO. Therefore, formulations below such as 'IGO influence' or 'IGO strengthening' are shorthands, referring more precisely to the IGO civil service as an actor.

I shall now briefly describe the reasoning for each step in the model: according to *the first step*, international anarchy entails diplomacy as permanent high politics. The height of politics as here conceived refers to national top-decision-makers' view of the area: is it closely related to perceived national core values (high politics), or is it not (low politics)? This can, evidently, be seen as a question of degree, and it may vary over time for an area (cf. Hansen, 1970, pp. 247-53). High politics is followed closely and *persistently* by top decision-makers (Presidents, Prime Ministers, or Foreign Ministers), whereas low politics will be left to the relevant issue-minister or delegated to civil servants, and only exceptionally it will catch high level attention.

In an anarchic international system, *relative* position in the international power/status pyramid is more important than the units' absolute gains, as convincingly argued Grieco (1988). The units' prime concern will be their mutual *general* relationships – i.e. those not pertaining to any substantial issue-area, but affecting each others' relative power position and autonomy (Mouritzen, 1988, pp. 41-46). The sphere of general relationships – here labeled 'general diplomacy' or just 'diplomacy' – will therefore *always* enjoy high level attention and, hence, qualify as high politics. Substantial issue-areas – be it agriculture, fishing, or whatever – do only *occasionally* win this attention – if something sufficiently dramatic occurs within the field. Therefore, they are low politics as here conceived. I do not rule out, however, that a substantial sector may gradually climb some of the way towards the status as high politics, even during anarchy; that is up to national top decision-makers to decide in the light, typically, of the nature of inter-state competition and enduring common challenges. Consider, for instance, Western economic summitry, the G-7 (now G-8) meetings, from the mid-1970s that heightened the status of economic questions. As expressed by Putnam and Bayne, 1984,

For a chief executive whose political fate hung on his electorate's well-being, international economics could no longer be considered 'low politics', left to bloodless diplomats, to cunning central bankers, to distant international organizations, or to the haphazards of the market...it was natural that the particular men in power in key countries in the mid-1970s would turn to summitry as a means for reasserting their power and responsibility (p. 8).

Military affairs have traditionally enjoyed high politics status (together with diplomacy often lumped under the ambiguous term 'security'); but that is not so by necessity. The only apriori given thing is that general relations will always be high politics during anarchy.

The second step in our reasoning links high politics to governments' uncertainty avoidance, which in turn means weak IGOs. It is, in fact, a commonly accepted hypothesis (Jönsson, 1986, p. 44) that influential IGOs are unlikely in high politics. The underlying thought mechanics of this hypothesis may be construed as follows: nation-states are generally reluctant to yield autonomy to other actors, including IGOs that they have themselves originally designed. In other words, they are generally afraid to lose control. A counter-argument would say that this loss would be compensated by the fact that other member-states suffer a similar loss. When we add to this the presumed collective gain in the form of better safeguarding of the IGO substantial values by more efficient and influential IGOs, the overall account should be obviously positive. It is not, however. This can be understood not only from realists' stressing of the role of uncertainty in international politics, but also from the concept of 'uncertainty avoidance' in organization theory (Cyert & March 1963 pp. 118-20, Thompson 1967, Allison 1971 ch. 3, and Posen 1984 pp. 44-7): organizations, including governments, strive to avoid uncertainty, also by the sacrifice of considerable benefits. Their decision-makers in general prefer

...alternatives with lower gains but also lower costs and risks to policies promising greater benefits at higher cost and risk levels (Schwartz, 1967, cited from McGowan and Shapiro, 1973, p. 187).

In other words, a considerable gain is willingly renounced, if by this uncertainty can be avoided (here: control/autonomy can be retained). This is a general phenomenon. But uncertainty avoidance is *especially* pronounced in high politics. In this area, the conceivable risks are so much greater ('catastrophes'). The gains are also, but again, the avoidance of risks is preferred to the winning of gains, ceteris paribus. In Grieco's formulation (1988, p. 499),

...realists argue that states are more likely to concentrate on the danger that relative gains may advantage partners [even alliance partners] and thus may foster the emergence of a more powerful potential adversary...states are positional [i.e. chiefly concerned about their relative position in the state system], but [realism] also finds that state positionality is more defensive than offensive in nature.

Or as expressed by Waltz (1979, p. 126), 'the first concern of states is not to maximize power but to maintain their position in the system'.

Given this cautious attitude, there is no reason for a state to run the risk that an IGO should weaken its position in the power pyramid, by its more favourable and efficient caretaking of the interests of other states (future rivals?). Even if it should increase overall efficiency, states seek to avoid any division of labour in high politics (Hellmann and Wolf, 1993, p. 9). In low politics, with lower stakes, there is likely to be more 'uncertainty acceptance', given the collective goods at stake. From this follows, then, more willingness to yield autonomy/control to IGOs. Hence, the latter will be more influential in low politics than in high politics, ceteris paribus. To put it inversely, in high politics, where top decision-makers are already unwilling to leave matters to their own (national) bureaucracies, they will be even less willing to concede autonomy and influence to IGOs. In low politics, government leaders relax their grips both on their own bureaucracies and the relevant IGOs and IGO bureaucracies (cf. also Karvonen & Sundelius (1987) pp. 10, 125). But the point is that they can tighten the ropes, *if they so wish*. This happens in singular crucial questions all the time or, in rare cases, as a whole area eo ipso is heightened on a more permanent basis.

As should appear from this reasoning and fig. 8.1, we are dealing with a *state centric model of IGOs*. To be more precise, it is a governmental control-relax model for IGOs (or alternatively a 'state allowance model'). In other words, their influence is seen as conditional upon the permission of nation-states.

Secondly, the model also asserts that this allowance/tolerance shifts markedly from one issue-area to another; it is neither a constant factor, nor randomly spread out. In this sense, the model is an issue-area model, predicting *varying degrees of elasticity in state control with the relevant IGO from one area to another*[3].

---

3   For some issue-area approaches, cf. Zimmerman, 1973; Underdal, 1979; Mansbach and Vasquez, 1981; and Evangelista, 1989. These approaches tend to be non-realist in their orientations, most outspoken in the case of Mansbach and Vasquez.

Fig. 8.1 A control-relax model for IGOs: state control in high and low politics

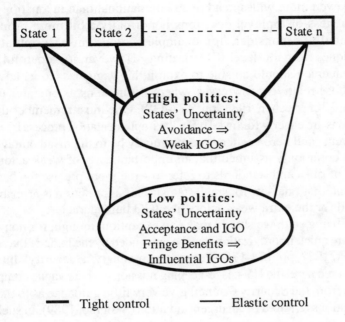

Thirdly, *the area of general diplomacy is seen as the one, in which states are the least permissive/tolerant vis á vis strong IGOs.*

These are three basic assertions of the model that were sought justified above. Fourthly, the model points to mechanisms providing IGOs with some *fringe benefits,* once they have been allowed to pass a certain threshold (being allotted their own implementation role and their own sanctions). I shall now briefly delineate the nature of these fringe benefits.

Low politics having made room for a certain implementation role and some sanctions of their own to IGOs entails some opportunities for their further strengthening (Mouritzen, 1990, pp. 73-76) – and hence widening the gap between pure low politics IGOs and those where high politics is prevailing. If it is allowed to have a common budget/programme, the IGO bureaucracy has solid arguments for subsequent control with its national implementation (a controller role) or, in a few cases, for carrying out the implementation role itself (an operator role).

That an implementation role entails actual influence is well known from national administrations: they can fill out vague frameworks of decisions, twist decisions in a direction unintended at the top, and so on. One's first impulse might be to believe that at least the former of these ways to influence would be even more widespread in an international than in a nation setting. The vagueness of toplevel decisions is normally a bit more pronounced internationally – consider, for example, compromise formulations in communiqués from top-level IGO meetings. However, it is doubtful that the IGO bureaucracy should be able to exploit this vagueness to its advantage, even in those relatively few cases, where it functions as operator (e.g. the World Bank, cf. Ascher, 1983, pp. 437-438). One must remember that IGO top decisions are eagerly followed up in the implementation process by *national* civil servants, and here vagueness can actually be to the disadvantage of the IGO. It is commonly assumed that an important asset of weak actors is the existence of rules and standards to refer to – the more precise the better (for example international law for small states). This assumption is probably even more valid for the extra weak actors like IGO bureaucracies.

This being said, we should make an exception, though, for non-routine areas, where quick improvization may be demanded by the logic of the situation (Lundqvist, 1987, pp. 174-175). Perhaps surprisingly, a 'security' illustration may be offered here: the UN peace-keeping missions, where vague compromise directives from the Security Council give very little guidance as to the actual field operations required by an urgent situation (Skogmo, 1989). In such areas, the IGO staff can temporarily acquire considerable leeway. Member-countries will not have time to interfere.

The question of implementation role also feeds back on influence in *previous* phases of the decision-making process. This can best be expressed inversely: if the IGO has little or no control over implementation, its position is weaker vis-á-vis the implementing member countries in previous phases of the process. It is more vital, then, that common decisions are reasonably acceptable to all IGO member countries, also those that intend to vote against or are sceptical. Everybody knows that they can otherwise neglect their implementation, implement decisions differently than intended by the IGO majority, or to a minor degree. Anticipating this pattern of behaviour, the IGO will be less ambitious and influential in its behaviour.

There is also another indirect effect from implementation role: involvement in the implementation process renders, over time, the IGO bureaucracy considerable expertise (including experience in the form of knowledge of precedence cases). The more expertise an IGO acquires relative to its member-countries (their IGO delegations/home bureaucracies) or other clients, the more influence it will get (Scheinman, 1971, pp. 202-203; McLaren, 1980, pp. 135-136; Ascher, 1983, p. 439; Jönsson, 1986, p. 44). Its arsenal of arguments will be improved: it will increasingly be able to refer to technical and 'impartial' arguments for its views that delegations will not always be able to see through or challenge. It should be emphasized here that it is not the technicality eo ipso of an area that is crucial; it is the *balance* of expertise between the IGO bureaucracy and member countries' bureaucracies (the expertise advantage to one or the other side).

Common budget/programmes constitute *positive sanctions* for the IGO vis-á-vis the potential recipients of programmes, that is, the clients (be they governments or non-governmental actors). Dubious administration or outright misuse of an aid programme, as evaluated by the international civil servants, may lead to a reduction in or a denial of future programmes. The potential threat of this nature can be assumed to be anticipated by clients and hence exert an influence on their behaviour. The significant conflict of interest is between conceivable recipients of programmes: programmes to one client passes by another one, and vice versa.

I have tacitly assumed here that the budget originates exclusively from member governments' contributions. However, the very possession of a common budget (and programme) makes it possible for an IGO to attract further donors (e.g. interest organizations, business, etc.) This would entail a diversification of its dependence (that is, not being wholly dependent upon governments). The balance of sanctions would tip somewhat in favour of the IGO. Consequently, its actual influence would increase.

In spite of the mechanisms described here, however, we should remember that not even the most influential IGOs can escape ultimate government control, according to the control-relax model.

High vs. Low Politics

Drawing the distinction between high and low politics seems to bring one into a cross-fire from such different camps as (neo)-realism, (neo)-liberalism, and neo-functionalism. It lacks the protection of an IR 'school' – a dangerous situation with the school-feudal structure of IR. Still, in spite of its being severely wounded according to its critics, the distinction seems to pop up again and again, apparently in good shape. I shall seek to demonstrate below that there are good reasons for this.

With the stipulation of the height of politics that was made p. 116, it should be obvious that I have avoided a 'substantial' definition, saying that high politics always refers to 'security' issues and low politics to, e.g., development issues (Hettne, 1991, p. 279). I think it would be unwise to exclude the possibility, by definitional means, that the height of areas may change over longer time-spans. With the exception for the *general* relations between states (under anarchy), it is actually up to government leaders to decide for themselves, what constitutes high politics. A conceivable objection to this 'inter-subjectivist' definition might be that the different governments engaged in an issue-area may not agree on its height. Which height should it be ascribed, if they disagree? My tacit assumption has been that governments, by and large, tend to agree; a government can hardly afford to downgrade an area significantly, if powerful governments see it as crucial. All governments have to give priority, with more or less enthusiasm, to issues that form the substance of inter-state competition, be it military means or economic capability, or to issues that form a common enduring challenge (e.g. of an environmental nature)[4].

A second objection might say that 'the agenda of interstate relationships consists of multiple issues that are not arranged in a clear or consistent hierarchy' (Keohane & Nye,1977, p. 25, referring to 'complex interdependence'). As mentioned above, dramatic low politics issues may win top level attention for a day or two. But it is empirically obvious that government leaders' height perceptions not only *differ* among areas, but also that they display a reasonable time-persistence. Even among NATO or EC nations, where 'complex interdependence' should have the most favourable conditions, leaders' perceptions converge around a certain hierarchy. For instance, it is obvious from Moravscik's analysis of the EC decision-making process (in connection with the Single European Act) that it encompasses crucial height differences:

> Movement in these areas (i.e. opening new EC issues, reforming decision-making procedures, and ratifying the accession of new members) requires active intervention by heads of state and a considerable amount of [nonbureaucratic] interstate bargaining (1991, p. 48).

In other words, national top-decision-makers do certainly perceive an issue hierarchy – with *general* state relations at its apex, as illustrated by Moravscik's areas (cf. also the height differences pertaining to NATO in the next section).

An attack from a quite different angle comes from the neo-realism of

---

4   On agenda politics, cf. Mansbach and Vasques, 1981, ch.4; on the question of a global agenda, specifically, cf. ibid. pp. 94-95, 103.

Waltz. His rejection of a distinction between high and low politics is based on the argument that 'in self-help systems [i.e. under anarchy], how one has to help oneself varies as circumstances change'(1993 p. 63), or 'States use economic means for military and political ends; and military and political means for the achievement of economic interests' (1979, p. 94). The former argument implies that new areas may become high politics. That actually supports the conception advocated here. It only contradicts the idea of a divine and everlasting hierarchy of issues. The second argument is true in some periods/regions, not in others; that is an empirical question. But it does in no way contradict the idea followed here that states perceive certain issues as more salient than others and that they allow themselves to relax a bit regarding the latter. The only formulation in 'Theory of International Politics' with a bearing on IGOs asserts that

> Though they [states] may choose to interfere little in the affairs of nonstate actors for long periods of time, states nevertheless set the terms of the intercourse, whether by passively permitting informal rules to develop or by actively intervening to change rules that no longer suit them. When the crunch comes, states remake the rules by which other actors operate (Waltz 1979, p. 94).

This sounds very much like the allowance-logic advocated here. Unfortunately, Waltz has not specified whether he is willing to admit IGOs an influence of their own in certain areas. His rejection of the distinction between high and low politics has blocked this road. Generally speaking, as realists find IGOs relatively unimportant, they apparently do not wish to invest their time and resources in studying these entities[5].

The distinction between high and low politics arouses suspicion in several camps. Realists apparently suspect that one wishes to reserve fields of policy for a power structure being different from the overall structure; liberalists claim that one wishes to subordinate all fields to 'military security'. Both suspicions are mistaken in the case of the control-relax model. All fields are ultimately seen as subordinate to general diplomacy – not 'security'. Still, low politics is to some extent delimited from general relations – but not in virtue of any specific power structure. States are just believed to relax their grips a bit here.

---

5   On the height of politics and neo-functionalism, cf. the EU section in this chapter.

'Security' and NATO Issue-areas

The term 'security' has been used in a whole range of different meanings: the use of military means, a policy that strives to safeguard national values generally or basic values like autonomy or survival (the latter perhaps the most frequent meaning), but also on occasions covering a policy managing marginal territorial conflicts (unrelated to the unit's survival). Furthermore, it is not uncommon for statesmen to declare that 'security' is being threatened, when they attempt to justify behaviour that to most outside observers seems to indicate that expansionist, 'imperialist' goals are involved (for some further uses of the term, cf. the extensive list of definitions provided by Buzan, 1991, pp. 16-17). In order to dispose of at least one source of confusion, I have avoided 'security' in the above model and in the book as a whole. Another reason is the survival connotation often clinging to 'security'. I avoid the primacy of state survival that realists tend to include among their axiomatic assumptions (cf. chapter 9). In a system of non-mobile units like international politics survival is only an urgent concern for certain unfortunately located units (cf. chapters 2 and 6). To be on the safe side, however, it is subsumed under the regime value of autonomy and under neo – realists' broader assumption of the state as 'defensive positionalist' in the power/status pyramid (*maintaining* its relative position in the system as its first concern). Non-survival simply means a zero position in these regards.

The exclusion of 'security' is precisely the reason, why it is all the more important to relate what is commonly labeled 'security IGOs' or 'security functions' (e.g. Everts and van Staden, 1993) to the model. That results in a heterogeneous picture. The conventional 'security functions' of deterrence and defence can be subsumed under the two traditional high policy areas of general diplomacy and military matters – being also the main errands of military alliances. Turning to such 'security functions' as peace keeping, peace enforcement, preventive diplomacy and peaceful conflict resolution, what they have in common is that they do not immediately pertain to the core values of those countries offering these services; from one angle, they can be seen as foreign aid carried out with unconventional means. That entails that they are not necessarily to be seen as the very highest politics; that, of course, depends on the saliency of the region in question to those countries offering their services[6]. Except at their very initiation, peace keeping operations in the

---

6   Operations involving peace enforcement is likely to be higher politics than peace keeping, other things being equal, given the likelihood of UN troops becoming engaged in proper combat.

past have not always enjoyed the highest level attention, not even in troop-contributing countries. The proliferation of local conflicts after the dissolution of bipolarity, with limited system-wide repercussions and, hence, limited saliency for most national core values, tends to reduce the height of UN peace-keeping as an issue-area (at the same time that the sheer number of operations has increased sharply).

It should appear from this that 'security' denotes areas of mutually different height. This can be further underpinned from the context of one single IGO. I shall briefly report here on my findings regarding NATO (Mouritzen, 1990, Part III). From an overall perspective, a 'security IGO' like NATO should not be expected to be influential in its own right, at least according to conventional wisdom. But such an overall perspective was seen as blurring reality rather than illuminating it, because of significant differences among NATO issue-areas. Instead, three NATO areas – those of force planning, infrastructure and information – were investigated in depth. Regarding force planning, it was found that the NATO International Staff exclusively plays roles in the modest end of the influence spectrum: co-ordinator among member-states, communication facilitator, passive mediator and observer, solely, in the implementation process (i.e. the defence postures being nationally decided and implemented). It was not allowed to *initiate* proposals. The modest influence that could be ascribed to it was due to its drafting of the socalled 'country chapters' and other written materials (the 'power of the draft'). In infrastructure, dealing with the construction of fixed installations in support of NATO military forces, the International Staff managed to play some more influential roles: active mediator[7], a strong expert and controller role (during implementation) and a symbolic role (i.e. infrastructure being the flagship of NATO coherence in virtue of its considerable common budget). But still, it lacked the most influential roles like operator (i.e. carrying out the implementation on its own) or initiator. These two roles, by contrast, were found in the information area – along with a controller role. In other words, some of the 'heaviest' roles were played in this area (seeking to 'educate' the public in all member-countries concerning the purpose of NATO and general lines of NATO policy). The rank order, in terms of influence to the NATO International Staff relative to that of national authorities in the area, hence, was the following: (1) information, (2) infrastructure and (3) force planning. As force planning, in line with a century old tradition, was considered the

---

7   'Active mediation' means that the mediator suggests its own independent ideas for the solution of the conflict at stake, ideas that are not just designed as weighted averages of the parties' initial positions, as in 'passive mediation'.

very highest policy in national capitals, whereas infrastructure was lower and information even lower (actually an almost neglected sphere), the sequences regarding IGO influence and height of policy were as predicted by the model: the higher the policy, the lower the IGO influence relative to national authorities. Even though exogeneous factors to some extent blurred the picture, it seemed obvious that the fitting between observations and expectations were due to the model and its intermediate reasonings. In actual fact, member-states allowed NATO to function supranationally, for all practical purposes, in infrastructure and information – actually little known outside NATO circles (and also a bit sensitive in relation to NATO's inter-governmentalist ideology). But still, nation-states interfered on a few occasions demonstratively in both areas, showing who were the 'real masters' – often regarding apparent details with national jealousies or sensitivities involved (e.g. how NATO information maps should depict some islands subject to Greek/Turkish dispute).

Regarding staff policy (ibid., Part II) – i.e. the recruitment and career policy for NATO international civil servants – member-governments normally prefer measures that safeguard their control over a quota of 'loyal' civil servants, at the expense of quality/efficiency considerations for the NATO administration as such. This national control obsession can be found also in the UN or even the EU Commission staff policy.

Paradoxically, in few arenas will one get such a vivid impression of the predominance of nation-states in the current international system as in the microcosmoses of IGOs. Within the limits of their resources, nation-states (their home bureaucracies as well as their delegations) try to exert an influence on anything that moves, sometimes in directions that are contrary to their own substantial interests. Uncertainty avoidance, the fear to lose control, is often more important than substance – even among 'friends' in regional alliances.

IGOs as State Instruments

IGOs and in particular those predominated by high politics were described initially as the 'twining plants of international cooperation'. The weakness aspect of this comparison has been dealt with so far. But two aspects remain: IGOs are surrounded by beautiful rhetorics, and they persist in spite of their weaknesses[8]. These two aspects are interconnected: it is this beautiful rhetoric,

---

8   The abolishments of the WTO and CMEA do not qualify as counter-examples to this rule. They are special cases, because their real members – the East European socialist regimes – happened to disappear.

not least, that makes IGOs persist. Nation-states wish IGOs to survive, even if they should appear redundant in relation to their official purposes. The reason is that IGOs and their beautiful rhetorics serve certain national vested interests, including beneficial unintended consequences flowing from IGOs' sheer existence as arenas of nation-state co-operation and conflicts. Hence, IGOs can be useful in less straightforward and more tricky ways than those flowing from independent actorhood. By way of illustration, the following nation-state 'arena uses' of IGOs can be singled out:

1) the IGO as a *face-saving device*. For great powers, to whom their (relative!) international prestige is always vital, IGOs can safeguard it in a difficult situation: the IGO can conceal a defeat, at least for a good deal of time, thereby making it acceptable. The classic example is the British/French political defeat in the Suez crisis 1956 that was concealed by the interventon of UN peace-keeping forces, making it possible to argue that the British/French forces had in fact been a kind of provisional peace-keeping force that had been set in until the UN force could be established. A recent example were the prospects of a strengthened CSCE and membership in western economic IGOs, which helped cover the Soviet retreat from Eastern Europe and to *some* extent save face in domestic and international opinion (Wallander and Prokop, 1993; Weitz, 1993, p. 347). The absence of the particular IGOs in these situations could have made the great power retreats too difficult to bear and, hence, have led to disastrous consequneces for world peace. The admission of Russia to the G 7 and the creation of the NATO 16+1 Council 1997 served to avoid a humiliation of Russia in connection with the decision to expand NATO eastwards.

2) the IGO as a *depository of legitimacy* (Boulding's formulation as cited by James, 1976, p. 87). The UN owns the biggest depository, by far, in virtue of the UN's universality. No regional IGOs can compete with that. But they are used, e.g., to confer legitimacy on various controversial great power steps, like foreign interventions. The US used the 1954 resolution of the OAS (that any American state turning communist would be a threat to peace) as a basis for interventions in Guatemala 1954, the Dominican Republic 1960 and 1965 and Grenada 1983. More broadly speaking, whereas a multilateral context will probably soften great power domination compared to a series of bilateral relationships, it also tends to legitimize it. For instance, it has been conscious US policy to maintain

NATO as a tool of legitimate influence in Europe in the wake of the demise of NATO's original raison d'etre (Nye and Keohane, 1993).

3) the IGO as a *tool of binding* of rivalling or potentially threatening national actors. The sudden enthusiasm of France and certain minor EC members in favour of deepened EC integration in the wake of German unification is the obvious example to mention; but 'Einbindung' of Germany is also involved in the classic semi-joke about the purpose of NATO: 'to keep the Russians out, the Americans in and the Germans down'.

4) the IGO as an *articulator of guidelines for (weak power) adaptation* (incl. domestic repercussions). The idea is that it is much easier to adapt to the 'legitimate requirements' of an IGO than to the preferences of one or the other great power. A government can use these alleged requirements to overcome domestic opposition[9]. IGO membership is not a prerequisite for this mechanism to work. On top of the unipolar power structure around the EC/EU in Europe since 1990 (chs. 4, 7), human rights norms as articulated by the EU or the Council of Europe have induced and assisted governments in many Central and East European countries to adopt Western standards. Future membership of the EU has surely been an incentive for several would-be insiders to adopt domestic laws and practices to fit Community standards (ibid.; Nicolaidis, 1993). The norm set being underpinned by unipolar power has obviously encouraged national adaptation.

5) the IGO as a *tool of dependency spreading*. This has traditionally been a weak power benefit from multilateralism, i.e. avoiding unilateral great power dependencies. It can be exploited not only within one single IGO, but also among them. For instance, the more Danish autonomy has been seen as challenged by the prospects for EU deepening and EU security/defense co-operation, the more Danish NATO enthusiasm has been mobilized. Likewise, much of the British WEU – enthusiasm has been explained in this way (Richardson, 1993).

This list of nation-state uses of IGOs should in no way be seen as exhaustive (for some further examples, cf. Keohane and Hoffmann, 1993). As should

---

9   This IGO use is, of course, sustained by significant IGO actorhood. For instance, the IMF with its considerable sanctions has been used frequently as an argument for unpopular economic measures that the particular government would have preferred, anyway.

appear, not only IGO members themselves may enjoy the fruits of these uses; also non-members gain advantages from a successful binding or face-saving arrangement, and the articulation of guidelines has repercussions on non-members' domestic policies. All of the examples mentioned here constitute vested interests for national actors; it is not the kind of values that are likely to be emphasized in the relevant IGOs' charters or official rhetoric. None of these vested interests have been principally aimed at from the very birth of the IGO in question; they have either been side-purposes (US influence in Europe) or hardly envisioned at all (the rest of them). During the turmoil of events, they have been discovered as *unintended consequences* of the existence of these IGOs. Being beneficial to one or more powerful national actors, their maintenance has *subsequently* been safeguarded for considerable periods of time. It is important to stress that this 'inertia benefit' is consciously maintained by nation-states, by and large; it is hardly the result of IGO bureaucratic inertia. As explained in the control-relax model, IGOs dominated by high politics are so weakly developed that there is very little bureaucratic inertia to hope for (as erroneously believed by Hellmann and Wolf, 1993, pp. 19-20). The socalled 'institutional rivalries' stressed by several contemporary analysts – i.e. NATO vs. WEU, or NATO vs. CSCE, for instance – are actually non-existent. With the partial exception of the EU Commission, these 'twining plants' are simply too weak to fight. What does take place, by contrast, are *national* rivalries over the roles of their respective favourite IGOs.

NATO bureaucracies, for instance, were not strong enough to safeguard their own organizational interests – such as task expansion – as the original NATO tasks tended to disappear. Only *national* authorities were strong enough to do that – and they actually did it (Nye and Keohane, 1993, pp. 119-20, stressing the US role).

In this light, the argument by Hellmann and Wolf (1993) that the persistence of NATO can be used to support Keohane's 'institutionalism' against a realist conception is invalid. Even if the perceived threat to the survival of Western states that provoked the establishment of NATO disappeared, the existence of NATO was still vital to member-states' relative positions in the international power/status hierarchy (expressed in such general guidelines as 'never change a winning team' – and even less dismantle it, 'don't rock the boat – it might send out the wrong political signals'). Secondly, the amorphous nature of 'threat' entails that it may be feared to return again on short notice; hence, the dismantling of the counter-alliance was seen as premature. In other words, traditional realist thinking is able to account for alliance persistence, by emphazising states' pronounced uncertainty avoidance.

In general, the difference between realists' view of IGOs and the institutionalist view advocated by Keohane et.al. (1993) amounts to a pseudo-divergence. The point is simply that realists are chiefly interested in the great powers, because they constitute the international system. And these powers' uses of IGOs are undoubtedly chiefly instrumental. The examples stressed by Keohane et.al. illustrating that 'institutions' can sometimes make a significant difference do all pertain to weak powers (cf. no.4 above) or a power that had just lost a world war (i.e. the 'intrinsic value' of IGOs to post-war Germany)[10].

Control-Relax and Theories of European Integration

The EC/EU is a somewhat peculiar international entity that hardly qualifies as an IGO. The ambition among its founding fathers was to get 'beyond the nation-state' (Haas, 1964) and create, in due course, the 'United States of Europe'. Even though this ambition was disappointed, member-countries have actually conceded a historically unprecedented set of powers to EC institutions, notably the Commission and the European Court of Justice (Burley & Mattli, 1993). In most areas of activity, the EC exhibits supranational rather than intergovernmental traits. This means that it represents a 'least-likely case' (Eckstein, 1975) for a state-centric model: should the idea of control-relax hold water here, on its away ground, there is all the more reason to believe it to be generally valid.

EC Issue-areas

Elsewhere (Mouritzen 1992) an early predecessor of the model at stake here was confronted with observations from three EC issue-areas, pertaining to the post-SEA period (SEA = the 'Single European Act', cf. below). The purpose was to postdict the national/eurocrat balance of influence in each area from the height of this area; the higher the area, the more national influence was expected and vice versa. With the definition of height of politics that was offered pp.116 and 121-3, the question can be described as follows: which national/eurocrat balance of influence follows from which national distribution

---

10 I am not saying that the interpretations of Waltz, 1979, and Walt, 1987, by Hellmann and Wolf are wrong; only that Waltz and Walt in some of their formulations have been unnecessarily restrictive in relation to the logic of their own thinking. Again, most realists' obsession with survival seems to be at the root of the disagreement.

of influence (i.e. concentrated at the very top as in high politics, or delegated to issue ministers/ministries as in low politics)?

The area of Common Foreign and Security Policy (CFSP) was selected because it represents the major EC attempt to break into high politics. It aims towards reaching a common position among member governments on various dramatic occurences in the world at large. It deals with *general* relations among states – not any substantial area in particular. The two other areas selected – the Common Agricultural Policy (CAP) and the Internal Market process (IM) – represent low politics projects that can serve as a backcloth to the functioning of CFSP. The CAP was the original flagship of the EC; a role today taken over not least by the IM process. The CAP's initial purpose was to increase agricultural productivity, to ensure a fair standard of living for the agricultural community, to stabilize markets and to ensure the availability of supplies and reasonable consumer prices (Marsh 1989 p. 148). Having come under crossfire today for its budget costs (70-80 pct. of the EU budget until recently), burgeoning surplus stocks, consumer prices and environmental problems caused by intensive farming, the standard of living objective for the rural population (the wish not to see large areas of Europe depopulated) has become the one that has 'saved' the CAP so far. The IM process was launched with the SEA (1986). The process implies the removal of various barriers to the free movement of goods, services, capital and people, so that one single ('internal') market can be created and maintained for the whole EC. The barriers may be frontier controls, technical specifications and regulations, or public procurement and state aids. National laws are being harmonized in the light of some 300 EC directives.

I shall briefly report on the outcome of the above mentioned investigation (but not go into details of operationalization). The observed influence patterns were as predicted by the control-relax model: the 'higher' an area, the less influence to the EC could be found – and vice versa. In terms of the model's reasoning, governments' uncertainty avoidance has left very little influence to the eurocrats in general diplomacy, i.e. what the CFSP is all about (at the time the eurocrats were employed in a small EPC secretariat separate from the EC institutions). As to the IM process and the CAP, governments have been much more willing to live with uncertainty: the Commission's exclusive right of initiative, the risk of being voted down, and judgements from the ECJ with no right of appeal. As a result of this basic strengthening of Commission influence, it has come to enjoy significant fringe benefits that are absent regarding CFSP: its implementation role has entailed the accumulation of significant experience and expertise that have further improved Commission influence. Also, the implementation role has given the Commission significant positive and negative sanctions vis à vis governments or other clients in these areas.

The EU in High Politics: Contending Predictions

As the EU ratification process was completed in 1993, the EPC secretariat was included in the General Secretariat of the EC Council. The Commission was entitled to make proposals just like the member-countries, but it did not acquire the exclusive right of initiative that it enjoys in other areas. An increase in eurocrat influence has happened – but in no way a dramatic one. The basic influence pattern of the pre-EU period analysed above – with much more influence to Brussels in the CAP and the IM process than in CFSP – is still the one prevailing. With little or no progress regarding common foreign policy the Amsterdam Treaty of 1997 has changed nothing in this order of things.

The question now is, if this pattern will persist also for the foreseeable future. Will the Brussels role in CFSP eventually catch up with that in the two other fields, or even supersede it? One's answer to this question depends on which basic theory one supports. I shall therefore briefly 'translate' the *general* control-relax reasoning to the theoretical controversies surrounding the EC/EU. As the EU is obviously the apriori 'away ground' of control-relax, we find more significant alternatives here than elsewhere to this way of thinking[11].

Control-relax vs. Spill-over.   Spill-over predicts that high EU actorhood will develop eventually as a result of an incremental process from 'below'. The spill-over model of regional integration was developed in explicit inspiration from the West-European integration process in the 1950s (Haas, 1958, 1964). Its idea has been analytically sub-divided by George (1985): functional spill-over refers to the idea that if modern, developed states integrate one sector of their economies, technical pressures will push for integration of other sectors. For instance, if an internal market is created as described above, it will be necessary to compensate those peripheral regions in the Community

---

11   I shall limit myself to nomothetically oriented ways of thinking and exclude, for instance, the post-structuralist/'reflectivist' school of thought. Even though spill-over, as described below, has its ad-hoc inspiration from European integration, it is obviously intended as a step towards general theory of regional integration – that may later be challenged by developments in Latin-American integration, for instance.

that will be disfavoured by this; hence, a common regional policy will have to be developed (e.g. Pedersen, 1992; Tranholm-Mikkelsen, 1991). Political spill-over refers to the build-up of pressures within the states being integrated in favour of further integration. Various elites within parties, bureaucracies, and interest-groups would shift their loyalties to the new centre and switch part of their political lobbying likewise. They would actively support the functional spill-over process. In addition, the Commission would assume leadership in the process, not least due to pure self-interest: the Commission is the logical future government of the emerging supranational state. The end product of this envisioned process was described as a 'new political community, superimposed over the pre-existing ones' (Haas, 1958, p. 16); 'nations forgo the desire and ability to conduct foreign and key domestic policies independently of each other' (Lindberg, 1971, p. 6).

As should be obvious, this flatly contradicts control-relax thinking, according to which states will never allow themselves to be circumvented in the way predicted above. The more or less elastic rubber bands in fig.8.1 would have burst. Not surprisingly, much of the criticism of spill-over has come from authors anchored in the state-centric (neo)-realist or neo-liberal institutionalist schools. The criticism that comes closest to control-relax as here construed is actually the classical one by Stanley Hoffmann (1970,[1966]) in the wake of the French obstruction of further EC integration. His main point was that whereas spill-over might well function in the low politics of relatively uncontroversial welfare issues, it would never do so in the high politics of foreign or defence policy[12]. In particular, the divisive issues outside the European arena being vital in high politics would prevent integration here.

Control-relax is able to live with the idea of functional spill-over, as long as it is not believed to challenge government control. Political spill-over and Commission leadership may occur in the sense that some elites become integration enthusiastic, but that will hardly affect governments against their wills, being dependent on much larger segments of the electorate (and being devoted to uncertainty avoidance). The empirical record tends to support this

---

12 'High politics' was defined ad hoc as 'matters...that go beyond the purely [EC] internal economic problems of little impact or dependence on the external relationship to the US' – having explicitly the French challenge to the US in mind. Apart from the latter, Hoffmann also mentioned the failure of the European Defence Community in 1953-54, when European unification was disrupted, as it knocked on the door to high politics (the problems of German re-armament). It should be added that spill-over theorists themselves watered down or abandoned their thinking in the light of EC stagnation – until spill-over was resurrected in the early 1990s with the new EC momentum.

view. Community building has proceeded in fits and starts through a series of intergovernmental bargains, rather than incrementally and deterministically (e.g. Moravcsik 1993, p. 476). Moravcsik's study of the SEA negotiations (1991) is all the more convincing, because it deals with an EC 'success story'. Hence, his evidence against spill-over ('neo-functionalism') carries considerable weight. Moravcsik's approach '...accords an important role to supranational institutions in cementing existing interstate bargains as the foundation for renewed integration. But it also affirms that the primary source of integration [here: high politics] lies in the interests of the states themselves (conditioned, to a large extent, by domestic politics) and the relative power each brings to Brussels' (Moravcsik, 1991, p. 56)[13].

The Maastricht Treaty process was even more a 'government control' story – both in the negotiations leading up to the December 1991 decision, and subsequently during the ratification trauma. This also appears from the very outcome of the process (Taylor, 1993, pp. 99-109). Popular attitudes – and their anticipations at government level due to upcoming referendums in several countries – were *most* reluctant regarding high politics issues – such as common foreign policy and monetary union (e.g. Nielsen, 1992). Nationalism, a phenomenon alien to neo-functionalism, was an inherent part of popular reluctance. This reluctance to leave the status quo was not only a popular counterpart to governments' uncertainty avoidance, but surely also a factor that reinforced the latter. It seems that the same government control pattern is repeating itself with the Amsterdam EU Treaty (1997); only this time, the outcome is even more of a lowest common denominator.

Control-relax vs. Calculated Amalgamation.   Instead of internally driven integration from below as predicted by spill-over, one can imagine EU 'high' actorhood arising at its own level, so to speak. If a sufficient amount of high politics collective benefits are in sight, governments will amalgamate or transfer their foreign policy powers to a new centre – be it the Commission GD 1 or somewhere else. They are not reluctantly pushed into it, as believed by spill-over thinking; it is the outcome of a cost/benefit calculation. The challenges from Japan and the United States – generally or economically – would make EU actorhood, entailing coherence and concentration of resources, the rational solution. Neo-realism actually holds a door ajar for this kind of amalgamation (Waltz, 1979 pp. 92; Grieco, 1993, p. 330). 'Only by merging

---

13   Control-relax in relation to IGOs is silent as to the role of states' internal factors; the main point is that *if* they play a role, they do so as mediated through governments. As demonstrated in chapter 7, internal factors are likely to play a crucial role for EU insiders.

and losing their political identities can middle states become superpowers' (Waltz, 1979, p. 182). The neo-realist 'The European Security Order Recast...' by Buzan et.al. (1990) delineate an 'integration scenario' (ch.10) for the post-Cold War Europe along these lines[14]. A parallel to the historic unification of American states has been central to this line of thinking (Wæver, 1993, pp. 34, 46-47). In the 'United States of America', foreign policy is actually completely federalized – whereas individual states have retained significant powers in various low politics areas. The EC influence patterns analysed above are turned on their head, roughly speaking.

Control-relax thinking, while fully appreciating the various incentives at stake, would believe them to be superseded by the units' uncertainty avoidance. A unit's uncertainty avoidance develops with identity. The more identity it carries with it – culturally, linguistically, historically, and in terms of an established state bureaucracy with its own organizational interests – the more it has to lose by amalgamation, so the more cautious it will be (i.e. avoiding uncertainty). Popular nationalism is, of course, a reinforcing factor in this regard. The American unification could take place, exactly because the young and mutually homogeneous states had not developed significant identities. But the European nation-states at stake here have simply had more than enough time to cultivate their apriori identities and, hence, develop their governments' uncertainty avoidance[15]. Control-relax thinking will therefore believe in the persistence of the present EU member-states as high politics actors. Should collective benefits be available in a given situation, these – or some of them – will be reaped through inter-governmental co-operation like in NATO or in the EU CFSP. Voluntary amalgamation will never occur in high politics[16].

State allowance does not predict any significant *roll-back* of the EU CFSP, either. That would 'send out the wrong political signals' and therefore be a too uncertain course (cf. pp. 116-7). State allowance therefore contradicts

---

14   The integration motive for some European powers might be less global in scope; they might simply aim at an 'Einbindung' of the newly unified Germany (ibid; cf. also Grieco 1993 pp. 331-35). High EU actorhood does not necessarily presuppose the 'United States of Europe'; Buzan et.al. clearly distinguish between 'state' and 'state-like qualities' (p. 204).

15   A few of these European state apparatuses/nationhoods discredited themselves through World War II (and later South European dictatorships). Hence, they had very little to lose and very little incentive to be cautious. That is at least part of the explanation for the momentum in European integration immediately after World War II.

16   But forced amalgamations as well as more or less violent state dissolutions will occur – as the present era in Europe provides us with so many examples of.

the neo-realist view that 'theoretical as well as historical knowledge tells us that a continent (a security region) can not rest where Europe is now. European integration will when exposed to the challenge of security pull towards either much less than now (1992-) or quite a lot more (1996+) [quasi-state formation]' (Wæver, 1993, p. 34).

While spill-over predicts integration and eventual high politics actorhood developing incrementally from below, the neo-realist integration scenario predicts calculated high politics amalgamation. In contrast to both and in contrast to wide-ranging political visions, control-relax thinking predicts no high politics amalgamation at all; the weakness of Brussels in high politics – in relation to national authorities and compared to itself in low politics areas – as analysed in this chapter will persist.

9 Theory and Reality of International Politics

Conclusions

The peculiarity of the international system in relation to other types of systems (e.g. an organism, a military system, or a market) is that it has *both* of the following attributes: it is non-hierarchic and its units are mutually non-mobile. This combination entails a unit/system cleavage: systemic explanation of units' behaviour becomes less fruitful than in other types of systems, as each unit will face a stable and specific environment instead of the system. Since power and influence wane with distance, this salient environment will have significant explanatory power in relation to unit behavior (foreign policy). The notion of 'environment polarity' – as distinct from the usual systemic (or regional) polarities – was introduced as a basic conceptualization for the salient environment. Historical and current examples were put forward, in which the systemic and regional polarities deviated entirely from nation-states' environment polarities, and in which the latter deviated significantly among each other – even among *neighbouring* nation-states (chapter 4). By contrast, homogeneity and stability prevail, if we follow one and the same unit over time. Of course, salient environments are transformed in the wake of major wars or state dissolutions, but the general picture is that salient environments keep constant in their essential traits for whole eras. Compared to other types of systems we have spatial heterogeneity in international politics, but astonishing stability over time for each unit. This contradicts conventional rhetoric of the form: 'the world is shrinking', or 'our country faces an entirely new world of unprecedented challenges'.

A few modifications to the argument should be made, however. Systemic explanation of unit behaviour may be relevant *also* in the international system in special regards or during special conditions. Firstly, it may be fruitful regarding the system's pole powers, not being subject to as deep unit/system cleavages as non-pole powers. Secondly, not all systemic polarities are equally powerless; bipolarity is probably the most hospitable one from the viewpoint of systemic explanation. Thirdly, periods or sectors of high interdependence

– as conditioned by technological and other background factors – favour systemic explanation, other things being equal. The fruitfulness of systemic explanation, however, is more the exception than the rule, even in modern systems with high interaction capacity[1].

The lessons for theorizing drawn from non-mobility and anarchy are farreaching but, by necessity, of a somewhat imprecise nature (as a pre-theory should be). Influential IR theories have borrowed their models from systems with no unit-system cleavage, unfortunately, such as economic systems (chapter 3). It seems that the systemic level of explanation shades the salient environment level in the IR community – whereas the latter is fully respected among political commentators, historians, philosophers, or in inter-disciplinary studies of war/conflict.

Kenneth Waltz' systemic balance of power theory of international politics is superseded by Stephen Walt's balance of threat theory: the latter can, inter alia, account for the prediction shortcomings of the former. This was ascribed to the fact that Walt – in contrast to Waltz – pays due respect to the unit /system cleavage in international politics, albeit unknowingly. Rather than a 'refinement', his theory amounts to a copernican revolution compared to balance of power theory, as the idea of an overall international system with explanatory power has been abandoned. Unfortunately, the Waltz debate has concentrated mostly on his explicit assumptions rather than the unstated ones – like the one that all units face one and the same system. Whereas Waltz's theory, after all, seemed to apply during the special circumstances of superpower bipolarity – because the superpowers were each others' salient environments – the overall structure has now, paradoxically, abolished its own influence for the foreseeable future. The unit/system cleavage is more visible during post-bipolarity than previously (but it has been there all the time!). In contrast to Waltz, 'Comparative Foreign Policy' and related efforts (such as small state theorizing) sought to explain foreign policy from pure *unit* attributes, mainly. By making unit-type the parameter for theory-building, they were blind to diverging salient environments.

In spite of their differences, however, what unit and system based approaches have in common is that they presuppose that there is no explanatory power *between* unit and system. This way of thinking is tantamount to a unit /system dichotomy of the form: 'if not unit, then system; if not system, then unit'. It seems as if the units were assumed to be vessels floating freely around

---

1   Even if the *explanatory* value of the systemic level is highly doubtful, it can be ascribed a descriptive/comparative value in a historical perspective, at any rate.

in the sea, so that their 'average' environment over a time-span will be the system as a whole. Predictions fail because of their common neglect of the unit/system cleavage in international politics. *Instead of a systemic (top-down) perspective, a bottom-up perspective on international politics is called for – but a perspective that does not fall prey to reductionism, i.e. explanation from pure unit attributes.* International politics is fragmented: it is formed basically through the interaction of related foreign policies. Some foreign policies are more related than others, whereas yet others are not mutually related at all.

It may be wishful thinking, but tendencies slowly moving away from pure unit explanation were noted in 'Comparative Foreign Policy'. Correspondingly, literature based in the Waltz tradition has departed from its overall systemic focus, inspired inter alia by the downfall of bipolarity. Variables have been added to Waltz's theory, rather than shifting the locus of explanation as advocated here. Still, from the standpoint of the basic argument made in this book a convergence from above and below should be welcomed. It would fit in with yet another convergence, the one between lessons from the inductive inter-disciplinary conflict literature (with geopolitical roots) and the IR adaptation literature.

Several theoretical constructs are compatible with the pre-theory of international politics advocated here. Three specific theories rooted in states' salient environment were formulated and tested in chapter 5. Whereas the first one was about 'tension between the strong and the strategy of the weak' (tested on Swedish and Finnish reactions to the New Cold War in the early 1980s), the second one was about 'balance of power between the strong and the policies of the weak' (tested on Finnish, Swedish, and Danish reactions to the Soviet disintegration 1991). In both theories constellation (i.e. basic set of relationships to the poles) functioned as parameter for the propositions. Within one constellation in the tension theory, increased great power tension led to an activation of behaviour; within another it led to a de-activation of behaviour. In the balance-of-power theory, constellation determined whether the weak power bandwagoned or balanced in response to the same salient development. The closer to a unipole, the more bandwagoning at stake. The third theoretical construct was likewise a geopolitical model – a simple one, indeed. This 'twin distance' model postdicted the five Nordic countries' different engagements in the 'Baltic cause' on the basis of their geographical distances from the Soviet Union/Russia and from the Baltic Sea region.

In all three instances, theories rooted in states' salient environments managed to account for almost all the empirical variance at stake. Individual countries display widely different (sometimes inverse) behaviours, although they are part of the same international system, the same regional environment, and are characterized by almost similar domestic and decision-making structures. The reason is that they face different salient environments, as specified by the theories at stake.

Whereas these tests were almost undisturbed by *internal factors*, this is far from always the case. What about the role of internal factors in explanation and theory-building, generally speaking? It was argued in chapter 6 that we cannot build a theoretical skeleton starting out from internal factors; the building must be based on the salient environment and then, if necessary, add internal factors in the light of prediction or postdiction failures. It must start out from the 'foreign sources of foreign policy' – from what foreign policy is all *about*. This external primacy was argued from states' non-mobility (once again) in combination with the established sociological theory saying that external danger to a unit entails internal cohesion-centralization. During a relaxed external situation, internal factors may be *permitted* to play a significant role as efficient causes. Statistically, it may well be that most foreign policies most of the time are driven by internal factors. However, the salient environment remains the permissive cause. With renewed external danger, the salient environment will regain control. The relation between the two sets of factors was formulated in terms of a control-relax mechanism.

In chapter 7 we saw two illustrations of interplay between a salient environment theory and internal politics factors. In both illustrations, the theory dealt with bandwagoning in the face of unipolarity: in the former case a unipole with predominantly negative sanctions (alliance theory somewhat refined from chapter 5); in the latter case bandwagoning in the face of a 'pole of attraction' with predominantly positive sanctions (the process of regional EU integration as already presented in chapter 4). In the former illustration, the refined theory was combined with an explanatory mechanism about foreign policy lessons learnt from past experience; in the latter, all kinds of domestic political factors were at stake.

There are other types of actors in international politics than nation-states. Even though a state-centric conception of international politics prevails in this book, it was important to single out the precise nature of this state-centrism (chapter 8). The control-relax mechanism which was applied throughout chapters 6 and 7 for a different purpose was reapplied here to the relationship between states and IGOs and states and the EU (a 'state allowance' model). States can control IGOs and even the EU, if they so wish. IGO influence is seen as conditional upon the permission of governments. However, this allowance/tolerance shifts markedly from one issue-area to another. In this sense, the model is an issue-area model, predicting varying degrees of elasticity in state control with the relevant IGO from one area to another. The more high politics involved, the less elasticity. The area of general diplomacy is seen as the one, in which states are the *least* permissive/tolerant vis á vis strong IGOs. Finally, the model points to mechanisms providing IGOs with some fringe benefits, once they have been allowed to pass a certain threshold (being alotted their own implementation role and their own sanctions).

IGOs are sustained at a bare subsistence level in high politics; on the other hand, even if nation-states are so reluctant to allow IGO actorhood, they will not let these IGOs perish. This can be ascribed to the arena uses that nation-states make of IGOs. A range of vested interests that states – IGO-members as well as non-members in some cases – can have in the very existence of an IGO were singled out.

A previous test of the model in relation to EC issue-areas was reported on. Its 'fit' was all the more significant, since the EC/EU constitutes the model's 'away-ground' – being a stronger and more ambitious international entity than an IGO. This made it relevant also to confront control-relax thinking with theories of regional integration: a neo-functional theory (spill-over) and a neo-realist theory (calculated amalgamation). Whereas spill-over predicts integration and eventual high politics actorhood developing incrementally from below, the neo-realist integration scenario predicts calculated high politics amalgamation[2]. In contrast to both, control-relax thinking excludes high politics integration altogether; the weakness of Brussels in high politics – in relation to national authorities and compared to itself in low politics areas – will persist.

Certain methodological comments have been made in passing throughout this book. However, after the above summary of the book's content it is now time to give a full picture of its methodology and underlying philosophy of science.

Critical Rationalism and its Realism

Karl Popper is the central philosopher of science in this century. It is not unreasonable to structure modern philosophy of science debates around Popper: Popper vs. the positivists (empiricists), Popper vs. the marxists and neo-marxists, and Popper vs. relativism (idealist philosophy of language, Thomas

---

2   Not a very likely scenario, of course, according to realist/neo-realist thinking.

Kuhn's philosophy of science, and instrumentalism in various versions). As a theory constructor or theory evaluator, one has somehow to relate to his thinking, whether one agrees with it or not. The school of thought that has followed in Popper's footsteps is labelled 'critical rationalism', a modern version of Kant's 'rationalism'. Unfortunately, this school has often been neglected or misunderstood within the IR community. Popper is famous for his battle with marxism, typically, but not for the other battles he has fought. Ironically, his way of thinking has often been subsumed under the general heading of 'positivism'[3]. An implication of this IR misunderstanding of critical rationalism has been that a first class 'weapon' against post-structuralism and its relativism has been overlooked; the 'outdated' schools of positivism or marxism have not provided efficient ammunition against this new form of relativism.

As has been hinted here and there, this book is based on the epistemology of critical rationalism, by and large. I shall justify this 'belongingness' in a more systematic manner below; in the process, I shall comment briefly on a range of issues that any philosophy of science must address. Unavoidably, this kind of methodological self-reflection will have a certain pharisaical flavour that the reader will have to endure; evidently, one has chosen one's methodology because it is believed to be better than various alternatives prevalent within IR and the social sciences at large.

Metaphysical Realism. This doctrine asserts that reality exists independently from our language and theories about it (contrast: idealism, relativism, instrumentalism). It has nothing to do, of course, with the IR schools of 'realism' or 'neo-realism' also dealt with here[4]. It is labelled 'metaphysical' by Popper, as it is not refutable as a scientific theory should be. However, arguments can be given in its favour:

> ...human language is always essentially descriptive..., and an unambiguous description is always *of* something-of some state of affairs which may be real

---

3   For examples of this misunderstanding, cf. Ashley 1986, Cox 1986, Keohane 1986, and Griffith 1992. Their 'positivism' label was applied to Waltz, but as his epistemology qualifies neatly as critical rationalism (Mouritzen 1997a), it is obvious that the authors in question do not assess the cleavage between these two philosophies of science as important.

4   For a surprising and unfortunate confusion of IR realism with metaphysical/epistemological realism, cf. Frankel (1996) pp.xiii-xiv. There are many IR realists explicitly laying a distance to epistemological realism, and there are many IR non-realists committed to epistemological realism.

or imaginary...Rationality, language, description, argument, are all about some reality... (Popper, 1973: 41).

A corollary of realism is the *correspondence theory of truth.* 'I accept the commonsense theory...that truth is correspondence with the facts (or with reality)', as formulated ibid. p. 44 (contrast: a coherence theory of truth and a pragmatic theory of truth that tend to characterize idealists/relativists and instrumentalists, respectively)[5]. It is important to stress here that the correspondence theory of truth does not entail that truth is manifest, i.e. that it is easy to get at. Naive realism is far from Popper's conception. However, it means that we can consistently operate with the existence of reality independently from our theoretical constructs, and we can talk about it without blushing or the use of quotation marks. In addition to this basic point, science should aim at *interesting* truth, not just truth (cf. 'The virtue of simplicity' below).

As should appear already from the title of the present book (Theory and Reality of International Politics), reality is conceived as existing independently from this or that theoretical construct. That means that for each theoretical construct, it is meaningful to confront theory-derived expectations with observations of the relevant segment of reality. In this way, pre-theories/theories can actually be evaluated and compared mutually as to how well they match the reality of international politics. That means that some theories can be seen as better than others; one theory can represent progress in relation to another (e.g. Walt vs. Waltz in chapter 3). This may sound self-evident to some, but it represents *a great privilege compared to relativism, according to which theory and 'reality' cannot be disentangled and therefore does not allow for any confrontation between them.*

Apart from theory-derived expectations, also theories' basic assumptions can meaningfully be compared to reality within the framework of metaphysical realism. It is a matter of contention, however, if and to what extent assumptions should approach reality (e.g. Koopmans' (1968) exchange with Friedman, 1968). Following Koopmans (1968), assumptions should not just be formulated as a basis for elegant theories with predictive and instrumental power; they must *also* be empirically reasonable themselves. Of course they should not be descriptively accurate (100 % reflections of reality; that would jeopardize simplicity, cf. below) – but in any case not the opposite either. Assumptions

---

5   The criterion of truth being internal logical coherence in the former case and practical usefulness in the latter case.

must have 'reality touch' in order to produce theories with adequate explanatory/ predictive power; the sparse observation opportunities in the social sciences entail that we can hardly afford the luxury of neglecting the realism of intermediary reasonings and assumptions. To put it with some overprecision, 'reality touch' should be about 70-80 % in order to provide the necessary simplifications, while at the same time resembling the mechanisms 'out there' in reality. For instance, 'economic man' with his egoist rationality is not identical to the average economic actor, but an opposite assumption that people were altruists would hardly produce as good economic theory as 'economic man' has done. In other words, formulating assumptions is not just an aesthetic/ instrumental game; if it is assumed as here that states are mutually non-mobile, that power wanes with distance, or that a control-relax principle is at work, it is because this is the way reality is believed to be functioning, basically. Even if assumptions are unavoidably theory-impregnated (cf. below), their truth is not theory dependent. *Any* viable theory of international politics must pay due respect to the implications of non-mobility/non-hierarchy or other assumptions. It does not suffice to say that they pertain to one type of theoretical framework and not to another; 'you can have your assumptions, and we can have ours'. Non-mobility is not 'what states [or analysts] make out of it', to paraphrase Wendt (1992) about anarchy. Its implications can be more or less significant depending on developments in weapon-technology, for instance, but *not* depending on our conceptual framework. Things can be done with words, of course (performatives); but that requires that they be spoken from a position of power and responsibility ('Our policy is one of strict neutrality' functions performatively if stated by, typically, the Foreign Minister in public *and* if accepted by the great powers). The general discourse prevailing, including that of the small state theorist, cannot formulate Latvia, e.g., out of her geographical location and its implications (not even the Latvian government would be able to do that).

With the view of assumptions advocated here, they should be justified one way or the other. For instance, the control-relax mechanism was justified mainly by the theory saying that external danger to a unit entails internal cohesion-centralization. This theory, in turn, has its solid axiomatic and empirical justification as reported in chapter 6.

The conception of language and reality as existing independently from each other also implies that theoretical concepts can be defined by the analyst; as distinct from concept essentialism, there is no such thing as the 'real' meaning of a concept (defined by the discourse prevailing among politicians or something else). For instance, it was argued in chapter 8 that the concept of 'security' is worn out for analytical purposes. There is no profundity in that, only the practical consideration that the concept has been used in so many different senses that it no longer conveys any clear meaning, but rather spreads confusion. Politicians' use of 'security' should be seen as political language with other purposes than analytical ones. That is interesting as an empirical object of study, but it is irrelevant for the analyst's conceptual equipment[6].

This does not mean, of course, that the selection of concepts and their definitions is arbitrary. Definitions should be made not only in the light of certain logical requirements to typologies (their exhaustivity and concepts' mutual exclusivity, cf. Rescher 1969), but also their usefulness as comparative instruments and, most importantly, their promises for theory-building (e.g. Mouritzen 1988 pp. 12-4). To return to 'security', not all dangers can be reasonably described as 'security dangers'; the EU threatens national autonomies (in return for its benefits), but in no way their 'securities'. Through the concept of autonomy, we can subsume dangers under one hat in a non-ad-hoc fashion; this is an advantage for theory-building. To take another example, a trend definition of balancing/bandwagoning was introduced in chapter 5, because that would make the dichotomy logically exhaustive and thereby also improve the prospects for theory-building.

Anti-positivism/anti-inductivism. One thing is that reality exists independently from our theoretical constructs; another is that this reality – or segments of it – can only be grasped through our conceptual/theoretical lenses according to Popper (belonging, thereby, to the Kantian philosophical tradition). That means that there is no such thing as 'facts' in and of themselves; all observation is 'theory-impregnated'. A good deal of Popper's philosophical efforts have been directed against the positivist quest for certainty, i.e. that theory should be built inductively 'from below' on a secure foundation of indisputable facts (Popper 1973)[7].

Knowledge cannot start from nothing – from a *tabula rasa* – nor yet from observation. The advance of knowledge consists, mainly, in the modification

---

6   Several concepts relating to states' salient environment are likely to be reformulated or kept silent by politicians, precisely because they are salient and thereby sensitive. For reasons of credibility, 'bandwagoning' will seldom be used by those performing it.

7   None of the philosophers of science that have subsequently criticized Popper have blamed him for his criticism of logical empiricism/positivism; none of them have advocated a return to this school of thought. This is the justification for describing empiricism as 'philosophically outdated'. Unfortunately, it lives well in many social science research practices.

of earlier knowledge. Although we sometimes, for example in archeology, advance through a chance observation, the significance of this discovery will usually depend upon its power to modify our earlier theories (Popper 1963 p. 28).

'Earlier knowledge' should not be understood in any puristic sense. Even if IR does not encompass established theories, there are general explanatory principles at our disposal such as those of role, rationality, or inertia that can be integrated into theoretical constructs, together with our various preconceptions of the field in question. The specific expectations that were tested in this book (chapters 5 and 7) were all theory-derived, that is derived from explicit sets of general justifications. In other words, apriori reasons were formulated as to *why* we should believe in the expectations (units' non-mobility, power and incentive waning with distance, rationality in the face of positive/ negative sanctions, external danger/internal cohesion-centralization and control-relax, units' uncertainty avoidance and the learning of historical lessons).

The underlying deficiency of 'Comparative Foreign Policy' research as criticized in chapter 3 was its inductivist orientation (cf. Mouritzen 1988 pp. 410-14). As formulated by the political scientist Harry Eckstein, induction is based on

> ...the belief that theories, being contained in phenomena, can be fully derived from observations, by simple inspection or, at any rate, sophisticated data processing (1975, p. 113).

By not formulating expectations' underlying reasons, very little could be learnt cumulatively from confronting them with reality.

The virtue of simplicity. Theories should preferably be simple (parsimonious): they should be able to explain much by little – by one or a few unifying ('simple') explanatory mechanisms (be it rationality, role, or unitary actor). We need a relatively simple starting-point for inquiry into the 'world of chaotic variety', to use Karl Marx's formulation. Popper is known for his quest for *bold conjectures* in relation to our background knowledge; we should aim towards *interesting* truths. This in fact amounts to simplicity: 'what is usually called the simplicity of a theory is associated with its logical improbability' [and, hence, its boldness, HM](Popper 1972: 61).

Parsimony urges one only to include those factors in a theoretical construction that apriori seem able to account for a considerable part of the empirical variance. For instance, the truism that 'decisions are made by men' (cf. pp. 21-2, 91-2) does not entail that decision-making or idiosyncratic factors should be included in theory-building, let alone form its basis. Only those principles/factors that formulated in a simple way seem to make a significant difference for our object of explanation should form the backbone of theory-building. In the specific theories tested in chapter 5, *one* factor (be it constellation or geographical distances) was able to account for considerable behavioural variance: activation vs. de-activation, balancing vs. bandwagoning, or high vs. low Baltic profile.

The more theories that can be coupled through a unifying principle, the more parsimonious the overall endeavor. For instance, it was seen as desirable here to unify the state allowance model regarding IGOs and the issue of environment primacy for state behaviour under *one* abstract explanatory mechanism – that of control-relax.

The classification principle regarding levels of foreign policy explanation was the stepwise abandoning of simplifying assumptions. At the salient environment level, we abandon the systemic level assumption that all units face one and the same environment (the 'system'); at the domestic factors' level, we abandon the assumption that all units react similarly irrespective of subgroup competition; and at the decision-making level, we abandon the assumption that governments react similarly, irrespective of idiosyncratic factors, bureaucratic factors, or factors in the very decision-making process. The control-relax mechanism and its underlying theory points to the salient environment as the basis for theory-building. This also provides a *simple* basis for theory-building, as prescribed here. Should predictions fail, however, we cautiously climb down the level ladder. This is the essence also of Wolfers' 'overheated house' metaphor.

Following the simplicity criterion, solely, one *might* have preferred the systemic level. Why not do that? Kenneth Waltz' main argument for this level is precisely the parsimony criterion at stake here. Obviously, most of us would prefer to explain 'much by little' rather than 'much by much'. However, if the simpler theory has the weaker explanatory/predictive power (explaining 'little by little'), our lack of an exchange rate between simplicity and explanatory power becomes highlighted. Then a metaphysical realist emphazising assumptions' reality touch – like the present author – will prefer the not-so-simple theory with greater explanatory power[8]. Assuming, albeit tacitly, that states are mobile and therefore face one and the same international

---

8   Waltz (1979, p.119) holding that assumptions cannot be true or false does not have this way out of the dilemma. His view of assumptions (Mouritzen 1997a) deviates from the metaphysical realism that I ascribe to him generally.

system is too far out of touch with reality (even if parsimonious), and it therefore also results in serious prediction failures as reported in chapter 3.

Anti-psychologism/anti-reductionism and anti-holism/anti-historicism. Unit attributes should seldom or never be given the honour of explaining system-wide attributes or occurrences (reductionism in its strongest form, psychologism being a sub-type of this). Popper repeatedly warns against conspiracy theories of society that seek to explain various unfortunate developments on the basis of the characteristics or motives of individual human beings or a specific group, functioning as scapegoats. In his criticism of John Stuart Mill's psychologism (Popper 1966, ch.14), he argues for the autonomy of sociology in relation to psychology. The preferred explanation of outcomes in the social sciences should refer to mechanisms producing consequences that were *unintended* by the individual actors involved.

One thing is that psychologism should be avoided; but we should not, following Popper, jump to the opposite extreme and seek to explain social phenomena on the basis of emergent properties of the whole, solely (holism). Even worse, holism may easily lead to historicism, the view that the whole develops deterministically according to its own immanent law of historical development (in contrast to scientific laws of the 'if.., then...' type).

The type of explanation recommended by Popper is situational (Popper 1961 p. 152, Stinchcombe 1968 ch. 5, Lukes 1973 p. 129, Watkins 1973 p. 88). Unit behaviour is accounted for on the basis of the situation *surrounding* units – avoiding both holistic as well as overall structural attributes and internal unit attributes, as a rule[9]. Following this logic of explanation as in the present context, international politics is analysed from a bottom-up perspective, but without falling prey to reductionism. To repeat from chapter 4, situational /environment conditions are the ones that are emphasized as the *interesting* ones in this type of explanation. To produce a full-fledged explanation, however, one must presuppose a specific explanatory mechanism (unit rationality, emulation, or whatever), a set of unit values, and a knowledge of the resources that the unit in question can mobilize vis á vis the environment challenge.

During 'relax', of course, the control-relax mechanisms opens up for internal factors as efficient causes of behaviour. However, that can hardly be seen as reductionism, as the environment retains its ultimate primacy. With the interaction of units in dyads or in regions, it is rather unthinkable that a

---

9   As argued elsewhere (Mouritzen 1997a), Waltz's overall structural theory is non-holistic (in analogy to micro-economic theory).

unit-internal attribute should come to explain system-wide attributes. Just as the fragmented conception of international politics advocated here is a barrier to overall structural explanation (not to speak of holism), it also makes the reverse explanatory direction improbable: that domestic attributes should have system-wide consequences.

As non-pole nation-states in constellations have served as cases throughout this book, I have not focused at dyadic behaviour (typically involving pole actors). Game theory is an excellent instrument to understand such interactive behaviour and its unintended outcomes. There is reason, however, to emphasize nation-states' vested interests in IGO arenas (chapter 8). These vested interests were often unintended at the time of designing the IGO, but were discovered as pleasant surprises in the course of events (the IGO as a face-saving device, as a tool of binding or dependency spreading, etc.)

Meeting reality: falsificationism – or what? The bolder the conjectures, the greater the apriori likelihood that they are mistaken, and hence, the more falsifiable they are. The more bold conjectures that spring from a theory, the more falsifiable the theory is, evidently. Popper's ideal is that science should progress (come nearer to truth) through a series of falsifications of existing theories, each time leading to the formulation of a better theory incorporating what has been learnt by previous falsifications. This ideal should explain the label 'critical rationalism': scientific progress (rationalism) is possible through criticism, i.e. learning by past mistakes. The doctrine of falsificationism was developed in opposition to the positivists' verificationism[10] and, as the latter failed, their scepticism (Berkeley, Hume, and their modern followers). Falsificationism has faced criticism in philosophy, the natural sciences and, even more, in the social sciences that I shall not report on here (e.g. Lakatos 1970). Eckstein (1976) and other theory constructors like Waltz have advocated a more lenient course vis à vis theories than that of falsificationism. Rather than consciously seeking to kill theories at the first, the best occasion, they should be given a chance of peaceful development – at least at the outset.

Instead of regarding a theory as falsified, deviations between theoretical expectations and observations can often be accounted for by pointing to 'disturbing' factors from outside. There were two types of deviation in this book (cf. also Mouritzen 1988 pp. 403-4):

---

10 The view that laws/theories could be empirically verified through induction. The insoluble problem with this view, however, was how to conclude that 'all X are Y' on the basis of a finite number of X observations. Falsification, by contrast, should be possible on the basis of observing *one* X that is not Y (crudely speaking).

1) *random deviations:* those that could be ascribed to the effects of factors that did *not* fulfill all of the following three criteria: systematic in occurence, systematic in effects and wide-ranging in effects. As an example could be mentioned the Nordic 'bicycle race' regarding recognition of the Baltic countries (chapter 5). It may have been systematic in its occurence (i.e. public opinion's influence on foreign policy immediately after the disappearance of a high politics barrier: the Soviet Union); on the other hand, public opinion is hardly systematic in its effects (it can push policy in various unpredictable directions), and in this case it was hardly wideranging in its effect (i.e. accelerating recognitions that would have come anyway). A deviation of this type is quite harmless and does not lead to revision, let alone falsification, of the theory.

2) *systematic deviations:* those that could be ascribed to the effects of factors that fulfilled all of the above three criteria. As an example could be mentioned the learning of historical lessons in the Baltic rim states (chapter 7). It was systematic in its occurence (during 'relaxed' external conditions), systematic in its effects ('success' leading to continuation of a policy, 'failure' to its opposite), and also wideranging in its effects (one country bandwagoning all the way into NATO, another just bandwagoning a little bit). A factor of this systematic type could be *added* to the basic theory of bandwagoning. Thereby, the theory's explanatory power was improved – at the expense, of course, of its original simplicity.

This systematic type of deviation (let alone the random type) did not lead to suspicions that the basic theory should be deficient; instead of seeing it as falsified, it was modified. If the basic theory has been formulated with an underlying axiomatic structure, independently justified, we would need significant and inexcusable deviations in order to consider the falsification option. We would then have to reconsider assumptions' reality touch and, more interesting, also that of possible unstated assumptions (e.g. units' mobility!). Also non-fit regarding 'most-likely cases' (Eckstein 1976) might lead to this consequence: a theory tested under the most favourable circumstances, but still leading to disappointed expectations[11].

---

11   By contrast, if theory-derived expectations fit with observations during the most unfavourable conditions ('least-likely cases'), the theory may, from a more practical point of view than that of Popper, be seen as corroborated (cf. the 'beyond the nation-state' EC as a test of the state centric control-relax model for IGOs reported in chapter 8).

Complementarism vs. Supplementarism Revisited

It should hopefully be obvious from the above methodological 'mapping' of the present book that epistemological belongingness is not just a kind of window-dressing, but actually something that makes a difference for actual research: the definition of concepts, formulation of assumptions, induction vs. the formulation of apriori theories, etc. One particular difference that I

Fig. 9.1 Supplementarism and complementarism

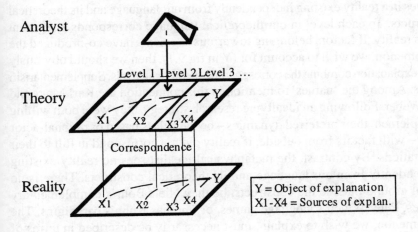

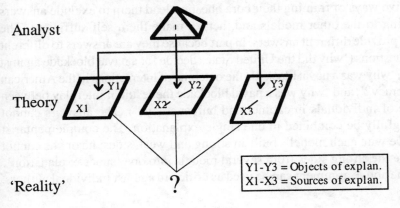

have promised to justify (chapter 6) is the one that I suggested between complementarism and supplementarism (cf. fig.9.1). According to complementarism, levels of explanation are self-sufficient; one can explain on the basis of one level or another, but each level is seen as producing a full explanation. According to supplementarism, explanation based on one specific level can be supplemented with factors belonging to other levels, if it cannot in itself account satisfactorily for what it sets out to explain. There has been a lot of IR disagreement (not to say confusion) regarding level relations (cf. chapter 3). In this book supplementarism has been followed (cf. chapter 7 for illustrations). That is because I am committed to metaphysical realism. I shall argue here that supplementarism follows logically from metaphysical realism, whereas complementarism follows from idealism/relativism. As a realist, one believes in a reality existing independently from our language and its theoretical constructs. To each level in our theoretical language corresponds a segment of this reality. If factors belonging to various segments have co-produced the phenomenon, we wish to account for (Y in fig.9.1), then we should obviously in our explanation combine the corresponding theoretical levels. Supplementarism results. Among the 'names' to mention in this connection are Karl Marx and Max Weber. Following an idealtypic research strategy, they were both willing to supplement their preferred dynamics – be they class based or rational-actor based – with factors from outside, if reality did not correspond in full to their expectations. By contrast, the metaphysical idealist sees no reality existing independently from our language and its theoretical constructs. There is no neutral ground outside the constructs, be they Niels Bohr's complementary theories, Peter Winch's language games, or Thomas Kuhn's paradigms. The phenomenon, we wish to explain, must necessarily be described in terms of one or the other conceptual framework (Y1, Y2, or Y3 in fig.9.1). Even though Allison's three models all somehow deal with 'the Cuban missile crisis', their respective ways of framing their core question lead them to exclude answers belonging to the other models and, hence, make them self-sufficient. The models provide different answers, in part because they are answers to different basic questions ('why did the United States decide for a naval blockade against Cuba?', 'why was a naval blockade the outcome of interactions in the American bureaucracy?', and 'why was a naval blockade the result of interplay between a range of individuals in cabinet and bureaucracy?'). The answers cannot meaningfully be combined in one single explanation. The complementarist must live with each model's built-in strong and weak sides; he or she cannot combine the strong sides from several models into one 'super-explanation'.

The above argument can be used as criticism against individual authors.

If the classification of Waltz as a metaphysical realist holds water (Mouritzen 1997a), then he should in the name of consistency take a supplementarist position – which also happens most of the time. But his *occasional* complementarity between his own 'structural theory' and 'domestic politics theory' is unjustified. Correspondingly, the distinction between a 'theory of international politics' and one of 'foreign policy' is, at best, hair-splitting seen from a realist epistemology.

IR Schools: Why Bother?

Interpretation of an author or a theoretical construct as belonging to a certain philosophy of science school has consequences in other respects. That means that the author in question needs to come up with some good explanations/ excuses, in case deviations from these consequences can be discerned[12]. In that sense, the school interpretation has been useful for research and not just a philosophical exercise.

By contrast, interpretation of theoretical constructs in terms of their IR school affiliation (e.g. to realism, utopianism, liberalism, neo-liberal institutionalism, etc.) is seldom a fruitful undertaking. These schools tend to merge a range of analytically and substantially independent dimensions, thereby making school discussions far too aggregate and crude. The inner logic of IR schools being weak, one is allowed to pick and choose elements almost freely from them, anyway. As I shall illustrate below, a specific pre-theory or theoretical construct may consist of some traits from one and some from another school, without being internally inconsistent for that reason. So why all the school classification trouble in the first place? School affiliation may legitimately be met with a 'so what?' question, since it can hardly offer prescription: corrections of past mistakes or guide-lines for future research. Secondly, IR schools tend to produce more heat than light, in the sense that school affiliation for some scholars tends to be an emotional affair — not least negatively towards alien schools[13]. Thereby, the reality of specific theoretical constructs is easily overshadowed by emotions of a more general nature (of the form 'are you for us or against us?').

---

12 Of course, anyone superficially familiar with philosophy of science discussions knows that certain schools are tighter in their logic than others.

13 As expressed by Goldmann (1988), '[These schools] are more useful for polemics than for analysis...The chief issues in the theory of international politics can be approached in a more fruitful way if we avoid defining them in terms of realism versus something else' (p. 1).

In spite of this, IR continues to have an almost school-feudal character. Textbooks, conferences and 'great debates' are often structured along school lines (school vs. school)[14]. Scholars or theoretical constructs not affiliated with a school have difficulties in catching the attention of the IR community, irrespective of their qualities. An IR conservative bias is obviously inherent in such gate-keeping. Sometimes one gets the feeling that contending parties in a school debate have agreed to have it precisely that way: translating or transforming their issues into school issues is a way they can hope to catch the attention of students and the scholarly community alike. We get far too aggregate debates of the form 'Can realism explain the new post-Cold War reality?'(e.g. Ned Lebow & Riesse-Kappen (eds.), 1995), in which adherents and opponents of this school, not surprisingly, stick to their traditional views. Or as argued (pp. 129-30), the difference between neo-realists' view of IGOs and that advocated by neo-liberal institutionalists amounts to little more than a pseudo-divergence, but the school labels function as drumbeats attracting a considerable audience. To take another example: according to a realist conception, 'the most basic motive driving states is survival...all other states are potential threats' (Mearsheimer, cited from Elmer (1996) pp. 19-20). By contrast, neo-liberal institutionalists assume that since survival is largely assured, the central problem posed by the international system is the lack of a central agency to enforce compliance with contracts (the problem of cheating that IGOs can alleviate). Again, what ought to be seen as an empirical question (whether survival is assured for all practical purposes or not) is treated here as general dogma. The truth as seen here lies somewhere in the middle. The units' mutual non-mobility and heterogeneous salient environments entail that some of them are located dangerously with survival at stake and others are located safely with no such concern (for whole eras and perhaps beyond). In view of such empirical heterogeneity, it is seen as wiser to include autonomy (that is always more or less infringed upon) as an axiomatic concern for the units rather than survival/security.

As a final illustration of school labelling, I shall briefly seek to relate the present book to IR realism in general terms. The question of affiliation is difficult to answer, because 'realism' denotes a school in its typical IR meaning: a loose agenda-setting community. As a necessary operationalization of its meaning, I shall relate to the characteristics of realism delineated by Frankel

---

14   However, schools may be harmless as *internal* discussion forums, as for instance in the twin volumes on realism published by *Security Studies* in 1996. These do not include the kind of mopping operations that one finds, for instance, in the school pluralistic volume on neo-realism edited by Keohane (1986).

(1996 pp. xiv-xviii)[15]: 1) states are the most important actors on the world scene; international organizations merely reflect the interests of their member states, 2) the world is anarchic, 3) states seek to maximize their security or their power, 4) the international system is mostly responsible for state conduct on the international scene, 5) states adopt instrumentally rational policies in their pursuit of power or security and 6) states rely on the use of force or on the threat to use force to protect their interests and enhance their security.

The present book seems to qualify relatively well on some points: nation-states, even though conceptualized as regimes, are seen as the most important actors in international politics (re 1). Their instrumental uses of IGOs that I delineate have an obvious realist flavour. Also, international politics has been formulated as anarchic (re 2), and states seek to maximise offensive as well as defensive power/autonomy (re 3), the latter being the basic value. Rationality (re 5) as conceived by Frankel is clearly an appropriate explanatory device as described in chapter 4 (although not the only possibility). And of course, states are supposed to use the positive as well as the negative sanctions at their disposal, if necessary; the negative sanctions ultimately include force (re 6). Under what circumstances it will actually be used is a question of instrumentality that I prefer to stay agnostic about.

By contrast, there are points that deviate from realism. Already the conceptualization of the basic units as 'regimes' instead of 'states' would probably arouse suspicion in some realist quarters (although realists like Niebuhr and Churchill clearly differentiate states according to ideology). The most serious deviation, however, is probably that the core realist concept of 'security' has been discarded here. I operate with a hierarchy of values like realists, but the top priority is conceptualized as 'autonomy' rather than 'security'.

There is also a grey-zone of points, whose subsumption under realism is dubious. The distinction between high and low politics is one such point. All areas of policy are seen as ultimately subordinate to high politics, that is (at least) general diplomacy. Low politics is to some extent delimited from this sphere, but not in the sense of having a power structure of its own. The units are just believed to relax their grips a bit in low politics (the control-relax mechanism), thereby giving IGOs a conditional independent influence in these fields. At least some realists, like Waltz (1993 p. 63), critizice the

---

15 There are innumerable stipulations of what 'realism' is all about; I have chosen this one due to its recent publication and since it functions as an editorial introduction to a volume on modern realism (published as a special issue of *Security Studies* and as an independent book).

high/low politics distinction. It is apparently suspected that the intention is to reserve fields of policy for a power structure that is different from the overall one (on the other hand, liberalists claim that the intention is to subordinate all fields to 'military security')[16].

Another grey-zone point is perhaps the most important of all: the preferred level of explanation. Frankel's point 4) is flatly contradicted here; the book's main thesis is that units' non-mobility, inter alia, makes features of their salient environment the main explanation for their behaviour rather than any overall 'international system'. On the other hand many individual realists, notably from before systemic vocabulary became fashionable in IR, would hardly object to this thesis. Moreover, the specific theories presented in this book operate with independent variables such as 'tension between the strong' or 'balance of power between the strong' that should in no way sound alien to traditional realist ways of thinking. Also, even though the control-relax mechanism may leave room for internal factors as efficient causes, the external environment is ascribed explanatory *primacy* – based not least on the sociological theory predicting internal cohesion-centralization in response to external danger. External danger increases the relevance of the sharp dichotomy between international anarchy and units' hierarchy (e.g. Waltz 1979 pp. 114-6). That should also be in harmony with mainstream realism.

Is the present book a realist one, then? According to Frankel (1996 pp. xviii-xix),

> Realists share these six assumptions, but not all realists share each assumption with equal conviction. There are debates among realists, the result of different interpretations and reading of these assumptions. There are even realists who reject or modify one or two of the assumptions (but then others may not regard them as realists).

According to such a tolerant attitude, the book might well qualify. The point, however, is that this does not matter for constructive (theory-building) purposes. The problem lies precisely in the tolerant attitude. One is allowed to ascribe significant explanatory primacy to domestic factors, there are balance of power and hegemony realists, 'offensive' and 'defensive' realists, structural and human nature realists, as well as 'moralist' and 'amoral' realists, etc. (ibid.; cf. also Miller 1996 p. 309). This means that the constructive guidance

---

16   To confuse the 'school picture' even more, there are works committed to realism (e.g. Buzan et.al. 1993) that allow for different power distributions between nation-states within different issue-sectors (pp. 30-3, 56-65).

offered by the school is negligible (cf.also Goldmann 1988, p. 13). After all, nobody can legitimately say, 'now that we have found out that you are basically a realist, there are one or two dubious point that you need to modify in the name of consistency'. By contrast, the school's influential agenda has even served to conceal really important dividing lines like the one between overall structural explanation and environment explanation, and it has diverted attention from (unstated) basic assumptions that misguide research. A bit humorously perhaps, the very fact that I have now come to devote considerable space to realism is an illustration of the ensnaring qualities of the IR 'school regime'.

Constructive guidance can be obtained at the level of individual authors and their specific theoretical constructs, when combined with the imperatives of logic and a specific philosophy of science and its methodology. We should focus at specific constructs, be it overall structural explanation, spill-over in regional integration theory, 'power wanes with distance', or external danger/causes internal cohesion – or at specific issues of contention, as for instance the importance of absolute vs. relative gains for nation-states. In the case of the present book, it should be obvious that Waltz's 'Theory of International Politics' functioned as a crucial source of inspiration. That is because this source constitutes a full-fledged theory (even if deficient), rather than merely a school. Erroneous predictions led to a search for unstated assumptions; the arguments regarding non-mobility and its implications in chapters 2 and 3 were developed in conscious opposition to Waltz's theory (1975, 1979) and guided towards an alternative locus of explanation. The fact that I share Waltz's methodology for all practical purposes made it easier to learn from the book's virtues, but even more from its shortcomings and the underlying reasons for them.

Bibliography

Agrell, Wilhelm (1983) 'Ubåtsjakter och opinioner', *Finsk Tidskrift*, vol. 108 nos. 7-8, pp. 362-373.

Allison, Graham T. (1971) *Essence of Decision. Explaining the Cuban Missile Crisis*, Little Brown, Boston.

Andrén, Nils (1982) 'Svenska reaktioner inför spänning och avspänning', in Heurlin, Bertel (ed.) *Norden og den internationale spænding*, Politiske Studier, Copenhagen.

Archer, Clive (1997) 'Security Considerations between the Nordic and Baltic Countries' in Heurlin, Bertel & Hans Mouritzen (eds.) *Danish Foreign Policy Yearbook 1997*, DUPI, Copenhagen.

Ascher, William (1983) 'New Development Approaches and the Adaptability of International Agencies: the Case of the World Bank', *International Organization*, vol. 37 no. 3, pp. 415-439.

Ashley, Richard K. (1986) [1984] 'The Poverty of Neo-Realism' in Keohane, R. (ed.) *Neorealism and Its Critics*, Columbia University Press, New York.

Asmus, Ronald D. & Robert C. Nurick (1996) 'NATO Enlargement and the Baltic States', *Survival*, vol. 38 no. 2, pp. 121-142.

Baker Fox, Annette (1959) *The Power of Small States*, University of Chicago Press, Chicago.

Berelson, Bernard & Gary A. Steiner (1964), Human Behavior. *An Inventory of Scientific Findings*, Hartcourt, Brace & World, New York.

Bjøl, Erling (1986) *Nordens Sikkerhet i 1980-årene*, Den Norske Atlanterhavskomité, Oslo.

Boulding, Kenneth (1962) *Conflict and Defense*, Harper & Brothers, New York.

Brecher, Michael (1972) *The Foreign Policy System of Israel*, Oxford University Press, London.

Buchan, Alastair (1966) *Crisis Management*. The Atlantic Institute, Boulogne-Sur-Seine.

Burley, Anne-Marie & Walter Mattli (1993) 'Europe before the Court: a Political Theory of Legal Integration', *International Organization*, vol.47 no.1, pp. 41-77.

Buzan, Barry et.al. (1990) *The European Security Order Recast: Scenarios for the Post Cold War Era*, Pinter Publishers, London.

Buzan, Barry (1991) *People, States, and Fear*, Harvester Wheatsheaf, London.

Buzan, Barry, Charles Jones & Richard Little (1993) *The Logic of Anarchy*, New York: Columbia University Press.

Chittick, William O. & Jerry B. Jenkins (1976) 'Reconceptualizing the Sources of Foreign Policy Behavior', in Rosenau, James N. (ed.) *In Search of Global Patterns*, The Free Press, New York, pp. 281-290.

Christensen, Thomas J. (1993) 'Conclusion: System Stability and the Security of the Most Vulnerable Significant Actor' in Snyder, Jack & Robert Jervis (eds.) *Coping with Complexity in the International System*, Westview Press, Boulder, Colorado, pp. 329-356.

Christensen, Thomas J. & Jack Snyder, (1990) 'Chain gangs and passed bucks: predicting alliance patterns in multipolarity', *International Organization*, vol. 44 no. 2, pp. 137-168.

Christmas-Møller, Wilhelm (1983) 'Some Thoughts on the Scientific Applicability of the Small State Concept: A Research History and a Discussion' in Höll, O. (ed.) *Small States in Europe and Dependence*, Braumüller, Vienna, pp. 35-53.

Claude, Inis L. Jr. (1956) *Swords into Plowshares. The Problems and Progress of International Organization*, London University Press, London.

Coser, Lewis (1956) *The Functions of Social Conflict*, Free Press, Glencoe, Illinois.

Cox, Robert (1969) 'The Executive Head. An Essay on Leadership in International Organizations', *International Organization*, vol. 23, no. 2, pp. 205-230.

Cox, Robert (1986) 'Social Forces, States, and World Orders: Beyond International Relations Theory' in Keohane, Robert O. (ed.) *Neo-realism and Its Critics*, Columbia University Press, New York, pp. 204-255.

Crowe, Brian (1993) 'Foreign Policy-Making: Reflections of a Practitioner', in *Government and Opposition*, vol. 28 no. 2, pp. 174-190.

Cyert Richard & James G. March (1963) *A Behavioral Theory of the Firm*, Prentice-Hall, Englewood Cliffs, New Jersey

Danish Ministry of Foreign Affairs (1996) *Rapport om dansk Baltikumpolitik*, Copenhagen.

East, Maurice, Stephen A. Salmore & Charles F. Hermann (eds.) (1978) *Why Nations Act*, Sage, London.

Eckstein, Harry (1975) 'Case Study and Theory in Political Science' in Greenstein, Fred & Nelson Polsby (eds.) *Handbook of Political Science*, vol.7, Massachusetts.

Elman, Colin (1996) 'Horses for Courses: Why Not Neorealist. Theories of Foreign Policy?', *Security Studies*, vol. 6 no. 1, pp.7-53.

Evangelista, Matthew A. (1989) 'Issue-Area and Foreign-Policy Revisited', *International Organization*, vol. 43 no. 1, pp. 147-172

Everts, Philip and Alfred van Staden (1993) 'Between Order and Chaos: Security Functions and Security Institutions in Europe', paper for the Second EuPRA Conference, Leiden, The Netherlands.

Frankel, Benjamin (1996) 'Restating the Realist Case: An Introduction', *Security Studies*, vol. 5 no. 3, pp. ix-xx.

Friedman, Milton (1968) 'The Methodology of Positive Economics' in Brodbeck, May (ed.) *Readings in the Philosophy of the Social Sciences*, Macmillan, New York, pp. 508-528.

Fritz, Charles .E. (1961) 'Disaster' in Merton, Robert K. & Robert A. Nisbet (eds.) *Contemporary Social Problems: An Introduction to the Sociology of Deviant Behavior and Social Disorganization*, Hartcourt, Brace & World, New York, pp. 651-694.

Galtung, Johan (1986) 'On the Anthropology of the United Nations System' in Pitt, David & Thomas Weiss (eds.) *The Nature of United Nations Bureaucracies*, Croom Helm, London, pp. 1-23.

Garrett, Geoffrey (1992) 'International Cooperation and Institutional Choice: The European Community's Internal Market', *International Organization*, vol. 46, no. 2, pp. 533-560.

George, Stephen (1985) *Politics and Policy in the European Community*, Clarendon, Oxford.

Gerner, Kristian & Stefan Hedlund (1993) *The Baltic States and the End of the Soviet Empire*, Routledge, London.

Goertz, Gary (1994) *Contexts of International Politics*, Cambridge University Press, Cambridge, UK.

Goldmann, Kjell (1976) 'The Foreign Sources of Foreign Policy: Causes, Conditions, or Inputs?', *European Journal of Political Research*, vol. 4 no. 3, pp. 291-309.

Goldmann, Kjell (1979) 'Tension between the Strong, and the Power of the Weak' in Goldmann, Kjell & Gunnar Sjöstedt (eds.) *Power, Capabilities, Interdependence*, Sage, London, pp. 115-141.

Goldmann, Kjell (1982) 'Change and Stability in Foreign Policy: Détente as a Problem of Stabilization', *World Politics*, vol. 14 no. 2. pp. 230-266.

Goldman, Kjell (1988) 'The Concept of 'Realism' as a Source of Confusion, *Cooperation and Conflict*, vol. 13 no. 1, pp. 1-14.

Goldmann, Kjell, Sten Berglund & Gunnar Sjöstedt (1986) *Democracy and Foreign Policy. The Case of Sweden*, Gower, Aldershot, UK.

Grieco, Joseph (1988) 'Anarchy and the Limits of Cooperation: A Realist Critique of the Newest Liberal Institutionalism', *International Organization*, vol. 42, no. 3, pp. 485-508.

Griffiths, Martin (1992) *Realism, Idealism and International Politics*, Routledge, London.

Haahr, Jens H. (1993) 'The Same Old Game? The European Community in the International

Political Economy', *Cooperation and Conflict*, vol. 28 no. 1, pp. 73-100.

Haas, Ernst (1958) *The Uniting of Europe: Political, Economic, and Social Forces 1950-57*, Stanford University Press, Stanford.

Haas, Ernst (1964) *Beyond the Nation-State: Functionalism and International Integration*, Stanford University Press, Stanford.

Hakovirta, Harto (1982) 'Finland in International Tension and Détente' in Heurlin, Bertel (ed.) *Norden og den Internationale Spænding*, Politiske Studier, Copenhagen.

Hakovirta, Harto (1983) 'The Soviet Union and the Varieties of Neutrality in Western Europe', *World Politics*, vol. 35 no. 4, pp. 563-585.

Hakovirta, Harto (1988) *East-West Conflict and European Neutrality*, Clarendon, Oxford, UK.

Handel, Michael A. (1981) *Weak States in the International System*, Frank Cass., London.

Hanrieder, Wolfram F. (1967) 'Compatibility and Consensus: A Proposal for the Conceptual Linkage of External and Internal Dimensions of Foreign Policy', *American Political Science Review*, vol. 61 no. 4, pp. 971-982.

Hansen, Roger (1970) 'Regional Integration: Reflections on a Decade of Theoretical Efforts', *World Politics*, vol. 21 no. 3, pp. 242-272.

Harf, James E., David G. Hoovler & Thomas E. James, Jr. (1974) 'Systemic and External Attributes in Foreign Policy Analysis', in Rosenau, James N. (ed.) *Comparing Foreign Policies*, John Wiley and Sons, New York, pp. 235-250.

Harf, James E., Bruce E. Moon & John E. Thompson (1976) 'Laws, Explanations and the X -> Y Syndrome', in Rosenau, James N. (ed.), *In Search of Global Patterns*, The Free Press, New York, pp. 271-280.

Hellmann, Gunther & Reinhard Wolf (1993) 'Neorealism, Neoliberal Institutionalism and the Future of NATO', *Security Studies*, vol. 3 no. 1, pp. 3-43.

Hermann, Charles (1969) *Crises in Foreign Policy. A Simulation Analysis*, The Bobbs-Merrill Company, New York.

Hermann, Charles (1972) 'Threat, Time and Surprise: A Simulation of International Crisis', in Hermann, Charles (ed) *International Crises: Insights from Behavioral Research*, The Bobbs-Merrill Company, New York, pp. 187-211.

Hermann, Charles & Gregory Peacock (1986) 'The Evolution and Future of Theoretical Research in the Comparative Study of foreign Policy' in Hermann, Charles F, Charles W. Kegley, Jr. & James N. Rosenau (eds.) *New Directions in the Study of Foreign Policy*, Unwin Hyman, Boston, pp. 13-32.

Hettne, Björn (1991) 'Security and Peace in Post-Cold War Europe', *Journal of Peace Research*, vol. 28 no. 3, pp. 279-310.

Heurlin, Bertel (1995) 'Security Problems in the Baltic Region in the 1990's: The Baltic Region and the New Security Dynamics and Challenges' in Joenniemi, Petri and Carl-Einar Stålvant (eds.) *Baltic Sea Politics: Achievements and Challenges*, Nordic Council, pp. 55-77.

Hoffmann, Stanley ,1970 [1966] 'Obstinate or Obsolete? The Fate of the Nation-State and the Case of Western Europe' in Cantori, Louis & Steven Spiegel *The International Politics of Regions*, Prentice-Hall, Englewood Cliffs, New Jersey, pp. 73-98.

Hollis, Martin & Steve Smith (1990) *Explaining and Understanding International Relations*, Clarendon Press, Oxford.

Hoppe, Christian (1994) 'Danmarks østpolitik' in *Dansk Udenrigspolitisk Årbog 1993*, DJØF, Copenhagen.

James, Alan (1976) 'International Institutions: Independent Actors?' in Schlaim, Avi (ed.) *International Organizations in World Politics*, Stevens & Sons, London, pp. 73-92.

Jervas, Gunnar (1987) 'Sweden in a Less Benign Environment' in Sundelius, Bengt (ed.) *The Neutral Democracies and the New Cold War*, Westview Press, London, pp. 57-74.

Jervell, Sverre (1996) *Barentssamarbeidet februar 1996. Hvor står vi, hvor går vi hen?*, Umeå Universitet, Umeå, Sweden.

Jervis, Robert (1976) *Perception and Misperception in International Politics*, Princeton University Press, New Jersey.

Jonson, Lena (1991) 'The Role of Russia in Nordic Regional Cooperation', *Cooperation and Conflict*, vol. 26 no. 3, pp. 129-144.

Jönsson, Christer (1986) 'International Theory and International Organization', *International Organization*, vol. 40 no. 1, pp. 39-57.

Karvonen, Lauri (1981) 'Semi-Domestic Politics: Policy Diffusion from Sweden to Finland', *Cooperation and Conflict*, vol. 16 no. 2, pp. 91-107.

Karvonen, Lauri (1984) 'High Level Foreign Policy Coordination: A Finnish Example', *Cooperation and Conflict*, vol. 19 no. 2, pp. 135-55.

Karvonen, Lauri & Bengt Sundelius (1987) *Internationalization and Foreign Policy Management*, Gower, Aldershot, UK.

Kaufmann, Robert G. (1992) 'To Balance or to Bandwagon? Alignment Decisions in 1930s Europe', *Security Studies*, vol. 1 no. 3, pp. 417-447.

Keohane, Robert O. (1986) 'Realism, Neo-realism and the Study of World Politics' in Keohane, Robert O. (ed.) *Neo-realism and Its Critics*, Columbia University Press, New York, pp. 1-27.

Keohane, Robert O. (1988) 'International Institutions: Two Approaches', *International Studies Quarterly*, vol. 32 pp. 379-96.

Keohane, Robert O. & Stanley Hoffmann (1993) 'Conclusion: Structure, Strategy, and Institutional Roles' in Keohane, R., Joseph Nye & Stanley Hoffmann (eds.) *After the Cold War. International Institutions and State Strategies in Europe, 1989-1991*, Harvard University Press, Cambridge, USA, pp. 381-406.

Keohane, Robert O. & Joseph S. Nye (1977) *Power and Interdependence. World Politics in Transition*, Little Brown, Boston.

Keohane, Robert & Joseph Nye (1987) 'Power and Interdependence Revisited', *International Organization* , vol. 41 no. 4, pp. 725-753.

Keohane, Robert O., Joseph S. Nye and Stanley Hoffmann (eds.) (1993) *After the Cold War. International Institutions and State Strategies in Europe, 1989-1991*, Harvard University Press, Cambridge, USA.

Kjølberg, Anders (1995) 'Norges Forhold til Russland og Øst-Europa' i Knutsen, Torbjørn L., Gunnar M. Sørbø & Svein Gjerdåker (eds.) *Norges Utenrikspolitikk*, Cappelen Akademisk Forlag, Oslo, pp. 318-339.

Knudsen, Olav F. (1996) 'Norway' in Krohn, Axel (ed.) *The Baltic Sea Region: National and International Security Perspectives*, Nomos Verlagsgesellschaft, Baden-Baden, Germany, pp. 116-128.

Koopmans, Tjalling C. (1968) 'The Construction of Economic Knowledge' in Brodbeck, May (ed.) *Readings in the Philosophy of the Social Sciences*, Macmillan, New York, pp. 528-541.

Labs, Eric J. (1992) 'Do Weak States Bandwagon?', *Security Studies*, vol. 1 no. 3, pp. 383-416.

Lakatos, Imre (1970) 'Falsification and the Methodology of Scientific Research Programmes' in Laktos, Imre & Alan Musgrave (eds.) *Criticism and the Growth of Knowledge*, Cambridge University Press, New York, pp. 91-196.

Leitenberg, Milton (1987) *Soviet Submarine Operations in Swedish Waters, 1980-1986,* Praeger, New York.

Levine, Robert A. & Donald T. Campbell (1972) *Ethnocentrism: Theories of Conflict, Ethnic Attitudes and Group Behaviour*, John Wiley, New York.

Levy, Jack S. (1989a) 'The Causes of War: A Review of Theories and Evidence', in Tetlock, Phillip, (ed.) *Behavior, Society and Nuclear War*, vol. one. Oxford University Press, Oxford, pp. 209-333.

Levy, Jack S. (1989b) 'The Diversionary Theory of War: A Critique', in Midlarsky, Manus I (ed.) *Handbook of War Studies*, Unwin Hyman, Boston, pp. 259-288.

Levy, Jack S. (1994) 'Learning and Foreign Policy: Sweeping a Conceptual Minefield', *International Organization*, vol. 48, no. 2, pp.279-312.

Lindberg, Leon (1971) *The Political Dynamics of European Integration*, Princeton University Press, New Jersey,

Lukes, Steven (1973) 'Methodological Individualism Reconsidered' in Ryan, Alan (ed.) *The Philosophy of Social Explanation*, Oxford University Press, London, pp. 119-130.

Lundquist, Lennart (1987), *Implementation Steering: An Actor-Structure Approach*, Studentlitteratur, Lund, Sweden.

Maclay, Michael (1992) *Multi-Speed Europe? The Community Beyond Maastricht*, RIIA, London

Mansbach, Richard W. & John A. Vasquez (1981) *In Search of Theory. A New Paradigm for Global Politics*, Columbia University Press, New York.

Marsh, John S. (1989) 'The Common Agricultural Policy' in Lodge, Juliet (ed.) *The European Community and the Challenge of the Future*, Pinter, London, pp. 148-166.

McGowan Patrick J. & Howard B. Shapiro (1973) *The Comparative Study of Foreign Policy - A Survey of Sceintific Findings*, London.

McLaren, Robert (1980) *Civil Servants and Public Policy. A Comparative Study of International Secretariats*, Waterloo, Wilfred Laurier University Press, Ontario, Canada.

Michalski, Anna & Helen Wallace (1992) *The European Community and the Challenge of Enlargement*, RIIA, London.

Michelmann, Hans J. (1978) *Organizational Effectiveness in a Multinational Bureaucracy*, Saxon House, Westmead, UK.

Miller, Benjamin (1996) 'Competing Realist Perspectives on Great Power Crisis Behaviour', *Security Studies*, vol. 5 no. 3, pp. 309-357.

Mintz, Alexander (1951) 'Nonadaptive Group Behavior', *Journal of Abnormal and Social Psychology*, No. 2, pp. 150-159.

Molin, Karl (1983) 'Winning the Peace' in Nissen, Henrik (ed.) *Scandinavia during the Second World War*. University of Minnesota Press, Minnesota, pp. 324-383.

Moravcsik, Andrew (1991) 'Negotiating the Single European Act: National Interests and Conventional Statecraft in the European Community', *International Organization*, vol. 45 no. 1, pp. 19-56.

Moravcsik, Andrew (1993) 'Preferences and Power in the European Community: A Liberal Intergovernmentalist Approach', *Journal of Common Market Studies*, vol. 31 no. 4, pp. 473-525.

Most, Benjamin & Harvey Starr (1989) *Inquiry, Logic and International Politics*, University of South Carolina Press, Columbia.

Mouritzen, Hans (1980) 'Selecting Explanatory Level in International Politics: Evaluating a Set of Criteria', *Cooperation and Conflict*, vol. 15 no. 3, pp. 169-182.

Mouritzen, Hans (1988) *Finlandization. Towards a General Theory of Adaptive Politics*, Gower, Aldershot, UK.

Mouritzen, Hans (1990) *The International Civil Service. A Study of Bureaucracy: International Organization*, Dartmouth, Aldershot, UK.

Mouritzen, Hans (1992) 'Agriculture, Internal Market , and Common Foreign Policy: Accounting for Eurocrats' Influence' in Kelstrup, Morten (ed.) *European Integration and Denmark's Participation*, Institute of Political Science, Copenhagen, pp. 213-233.

Mouritzen, Hans (1996a) 'Comparative and Theoretical Insights', pp. 261-77 in Mouritzen, Hans, Ole Wæver & Håkan Wiberg (1996) *European Integration and National Adaptation: A Theoretical Inquiry*, Nova Science Publishers, New York.

Mouritzen, Hans (1996b) 'Polarity and Constellations', pp. 17-26 in Mouritzen, Hans, Ole Wæver & Håkan Wiberg (1996) *European Integration and National Adaptation: A Theoretical Inquiry*, Nova Science Publishers, New York.

Mouritzen, Hans (1997a) 'Kenneth Waltz: a Critical Rationalist between International Politics and Foreign Policy' in Neumann, Iver & Ole Wæver (eds.) *The Future of International Relations. Masters in the Making ?*, Routledge, London, pp.66-90.

Mouritzen , Hans (1997b) *External Danger and Democracy: Old Nordic Lessons and New European Challenges*, Dartmouth, Aldershot, UK.

Mouritzen, Hans (1998) (ed.) *Bordering Russia: Theory and Prospects for Europe's Baltic Rim*, Ashgate, Aldershot, UK.

Mouritzen, Hans, Ole Wæver & Håkan Wiberg (1996) *European Integration and National Adaptation: A Theoretical Inquiry*, Nova Science Publishers, New York.

Nicolaïdes, Kalypso (1993) 'East European Trade in the Aftermath of 1989: Did International Institutions Matter' in Keohane, Robert O., Joseph S. Nye & Stanley Hoffmann (eds.) *After the Cold War. International Institutions and State Strategies in Europe, 1989-1991*, Harvard University Press, Cambridge, USA, pp. 197-245.

Nielsen, Hans Jørgen (1992) 'The Danish Voters and the Referendum in June 1992 on the Maastricht Agreement'in Kelstrup, Morten (ed.) *European Integration and Denmark's Participation*, Copenhagen Institute of Political Science, Copenhagen , pp. 365-381.

Nielsson, Gunnar P. (1990) 'The parallel national action process' in Groom, A.J.R & Paul Taylor *Frameworks for International Cooperation*, Pinter Publishers, London, pp. 79-108.

Nye, Joseph S. & Robert O. Keohane 'The United States and International Institutions in Europe After the Cold War' in Keohane, Robert O., Joseph S. Nye & Stanley Hoffmann (eds.) *After the Cold War. International Institutions and State Strategies in Europe, 1989-1991*, Harvard University Press, Cambridge, USA, pp. 104-126.

O'Sullivan, Patrick (1986), *Geopolitics*, Croom Helm, London.

Oye, Kenneth A. (1985) 'Explaining Cooperation under Anarchy: Hypotheses and Strategies', *World Politics*, vol. 38 no. 1, pp. 1-24.

Ozolina, Zaneta (1996) 'The Nordic and the Baltic Countries: A Sub-Region in the Making?' in Leijins, Atis & Daina Bleiere (eds.) *The Baltic States. Search for Security*, Latvian Institute of International Affairs, Riga, pp. 93-111.

Palme, Olof et al. (1982) Common Security. *The Palme Commision Report*, Pan, London.

Papadakis, Maria & Harvey Starr (1987) 'Opportunity, Willingness and Small States: The Relationship Between Environment and Foreign Policy' in Hermann, Charles F, Charles W. Kegley, Jr. & James N. Rosenau (eds.) *New Directions in the Study of Foreign Policy*, Unwin Hyman, Boston, pp. 409-432.

Pedersen, Thomas (1992) 'Political Change in the EC. The SEA as a Case of System Transformation' in Kelstrup, Morten (ed.) *European Integration and Denmark's Participation*, Institute of Political Science, Copenhagen, pp. 184-213.

Penttilä, Risto (1991), *Finland's Search for Security through Defence 1944-89*, St. Martin's Press, London.

Petersen, Nikolaj (1977) 'Adaptation as a Framework for Foreign Policy Behaviour', *Cooperation and Conflict*, vol. 12 no. 4, pp. 221-250.

Popper, Karl (1961) [1957] *The Poverty of Historicism*, Routledge, London.

Popper, Karl (1966) [1945] *The Open Society and its Enemies*, Routledge, London.

Popper, Karl (1972) [1963] *Conjectures and Refutations*, Routledge, London.

Popper, Karl (1973) [1972] *Objective Knowledge*, Oxford University Press, London.

Posen, Barry (1984) *The Sources of Military Doctrine. France, Britain and Germany between the World Wars*, Cornell University Press, Ithaca and London.

Poulsen-Hansen, Lars & Ole Wæver (1996) "The Ukraine" in Mouritzen, Hans, Ole Wæver & Håkan Wiberg (eds.) *European Integration and National Adaptation: A Theoretical Inquiry*, Nova Science Publishers, New York, pp. 231-261.

Putnam, Robert & N. Bayne (1984) *Hanging Together. The Seven-Power Summits*, Heinemann for RIIA, London.

Rescher, Nicholas (1969) *Introduction to Logic*, New York.

Richardson Louise (1993) 'British State Strategies After the Cold War' in Keohane, Robert O., Joseph S. Nye & Stanley Hoffmann (eds.) *After the Cold War. International Institutions and State Strategies in Europe, 1989-1991*, Harvard University Press, Cambridge, USA, pp. 148-171.

Rosecrance, Richard (1963) *Action and Reaction in World Politics*, Little Brown, Boston.

Rosenau, James, 1980 [1966] 'Pre-theories and Theories of Foreign Policy' in Rosenau, James N. *The Scientific Study of Foreign Policy*, rev. ed., Francis Pinter, London, pp. 115-170.

Rosenau, James N. (1967) "Compatibility, Consensus, and an Emerging Political Science of Adaptation", *American Political Science Review*, vol. 61 no.4, pp. 983-988.

Rosenau, James N., with Gary Hoggard (1974) 'Foreign Policy Behavior in Dyadic Relationsships: Testing a Pre-Theoretical Extension'. in Rosenau, James N. (ed.), *Comparing Foreign Policies*, John Wiley and Sons, New York, pp. 117-150.

Rosenau, James N., with George Ramsey (1980) 'External and Internal Typologies of Foreign Policy Behavior' in Rosenau, James N., *The Scientific Study of Foreign Policy*, rev. ed., Francis Pinter, London, pp. 213-230.

Rothstein, Robert (1968) *Alliances and Small Powers*, Columbia University Press, New York.

Ruggie, John G. (1986) 'Continuity and Transformation in the World Polity: Towards a Neorealist Synthesis', in Robert O.Keohane (ed.) *Neorealism and its Critics*, Columbia University Press, New York, pp. 131-158.

Rummel, Rudolph (1969) 'Some Dimensions in the Foreign Behavior of Nations' in James N. Rosenau (ed.) *International Politics and Foreign Policies*, Free Press, New York, pp. 600-621.

Samuelsson, Per (1996) *Svensk syn på Baltikums frigörelse 1988-1996*, FOA, Stockholm.

Scheinman, Lawrence (1971) 'Economic Regionalism and International Administration: The European Communities Experience' in Jordan, Robert S. (ed.) *International Administration. Its Evaluation and Contemporary Applications*, Oxford University Press, London, pp. 187-227.

Schwartz, David C. (1967) 'Decision Theories and Crisis Behavior: An Empirical Study of Nuclear Deterrence in International Political Crises', *Orbis*, vol. 11 no. 2, pp. 459-490.

Singer, David (1961) 'The Level-of-Analysis Problem in International Relations' in Knorr, Klaus & Sidney Verba (eds.) *The International System: Theoretical Essays*, Princeton University Press, New Jersey.

Sjöblom, Gunnar (1968) *Party Strategies in a Multiparty System*, Studentlitteratur, Lund, Sweden.

Skogmo, Bjørn (1989) *International Peacekeeping in Lebanon, 1978-1988*, Lynne Rienner, London.

Smith, Steve (1981) *Foreign Policy Adaptation*, Gower, Aldershot, England.

Snyder, Glenn H. (1984) 'The Security Dilemma in Alliance Politics', *World Politics*, July, pp. 461-495.

Snyder, Jack & Robert Jervis (eds.) (1993) *Coping with Complexity in the International System*, Westview Press, Boulder, USA.

Soikkanen, Hannu (1979) 'Sociala förhallanden' in Molin, Karl et al. *Norden under andra världskriget*. Gyldendal, Copenhagen, pp. 105-135.

SOU (1983) *Att möta ubåtshotet. Ubåtskränkningar och svensk säkerhetspolitik*, Statens Offentliga Utredningar, Stockholm.

Spanier, John W. (1972) *Games Nations Play*, Praeger, London.

Sprout, Harold & Margaret Sprout (1956) *Man-Mileu Relationship Hypotheses in the Context of International Politics*, Center for International Studies, Princeton University, New Jersey.

Spykman, Nicholas (1942) *America's Strategy in World Politics. The United States and the*

Balance of Power, Harcourt, New York.

Stein, Arthur A. (1976) 'Conflict and Cohesion. A Review of Literature', *Journal of Conflict Resolution*, vol. 20 no. 1, pp. 143-172.

Stein, Janice G. (1996) 'Deterrence and Learning in an Enduring Rivalry: Egypt and Israel, 1948-73', *Security Studies*, vol. 6 no. 1, pp. 104-152.

Steinbruner, John D. (1974) *The Cybernetic Theory of Decision. New Dimensions of Political Analysis*, Princeton, New Jersey.

Stenelo, Lars Göran (1981) 'Prediction and Foreign Policy Heritage' in *Cooperation and Conflict*, no. 1, pp. 3-19.

Stinchcombe, Arthur L. (1968) *Constructing Social Theories*, Hartcourt, Brace & World, New York.

Subtelny, Orest (1988) *Ukraine: A History*, University of Toronto Press, Toronto.

Sundelius, Bengt (1994) 'Changing Course: When Neutral Sweden Chose to Join the European Community', in Carlsnaes, Walter & Steve Smith (eds.) *European Foreign Policy. The EC and Changing Perspectives in Europe*, Sage, London, pp. 177-201.

Sylvan, David & Barry Glasner (1985) *A Rationalist Methodology for the Social Sciences*, Basil Blackwell, Oxford.

Taylor, Paul (1993) *International Organization in the Modern World*, Pinter, London.

Tellis, Ashley J. (1996) 'Reconstructing Political Realism: The Long March to Scientific Theory', *Security Studies*, vol. 5 no. 2, pp. 3-105.

Thompson, James D. (1967) *Organizations in Action*, McGraw-Hill, New York.

Tranholm-Mikkelsen, Jeppe (1991) 'Neo-functionalism: Obstinate or Obsolete? A Reappraisal in the Light of the New Dynamism of the EC', *Millennium*, vol. 20 no.1, pp. 1-22.

Tunander, Ola (1989) *Cold Water Politics. The Maritime Strategy and Geopolitics of the Northern Front*, Sage, London.

Tunander, Ola (1995) 'Norge og Norden' i Knutsen, Torbjørn L., Gunnar M. Sørbø & Svein Gjerdåker (eds.) *Norges Utenrikspolitikk*, Cappelen Akademisk Forlag, Oslo, pp. 260-277.

Underdal, Arild (1979) 'Issues Determine Politics Determine Policies: The Case for a 'Rationalistic' Approach to the Study of Foreign Policy Decision-Making', *Cooperation and Conflict*, vol. 14 no. 1, pp. 1-10.

Vikström, Lars (1996) 'Sverige tar ledarroll i Östersjöpolitiken', *Ny Tid*, September 6.

Vital, David (1971) *The Survival of Small States. Studies in Small Power/Great Power Conflict*, Oxford University Press, London.

Vloyantes, John (1975) *Silk Glove Hegemony: Finnish-Soviet Relations, 1944-64*, Kent, Ohio.

Väyrynen, Raimo (1972) *Conflicts in Finnish-Soviet Relations: Three Comparative Case-studies*, ser. A vol. 47, Acta Universitatis Tamperensis, Tampere, Finland.

Väyrynen, Raimo (1983) 'Den utrikespolitiska diskussionen og beslutsfattandet i Finland under Koivistos mandatperiod', *Internasjonal Politikk*, vol. 41 no. 2, pp. 155-168.

Väyrynen, Raimo (1987) 'Adaptation of a Small Power to International Tensions: The Case of Finland' in Sundelius, Bengt, (ed.) *The Neutral Democracies and the New Cold War* Westview Press, London, pp. 33-56.

Wallander, Celleste & Jane Prokop (1993) 'Soviet Security Strategies toward Europe: After the Wall with Their Backs up against It' in Keohane, Robert O., Joseph S. Nye & Stanley Hoffmann (eds.) *After the Cold War. International Institutions and State Strategies in Europe, 1989-1991*, Harvard University Press, Cambridge, USA, pp. 63-103.

Walt, Stephen (1987) *The Origins of Alliances*, Cornell University Press, Ithaca, USA.

Walt, Stephen (1988) 'Testing theories of alliance formation: the case of Southwest Asia', *International Organization*, vol. 42 no. 2, pp. 275-316.

Walt, Stephen (1992) 'Alliance, Threats, and the U.S. Grand Strategy: A Reply to Kaufmann and Labs', *Security Studies*, vol. 1 no. 3, pp. 448-482.

Waltz, Kenneth (1959) *Man, State and War*, Columbia University Press, New York.

Waltz, Kenneth (1975) 'Theory of International Relations' in Greenstein, Fred I. & Nelson W. Polsby (eds.), *International Politics, Handbook of Political Science*, Vol 8, Addison-Wesley, Reading, USA, pp. 1-85.

Waltz, Kenneth (1979) *Theory of International Politics*, Random House, New York.

Waltz, Kenneth (1990) 'Realist Thought and Neorealist Theory', *Journal of International Affairs*, vol. 44 no. 1, pp. 21-37.

Waltz, Kenneth (1993) 'The Emerging Structure of International Politics', *International Security*, vol. 18 no. 2, pp. 44-79.

Watkins, James L. (1973) 'Ideal Types and Historical Explanation' in Ryan, Alan (ed.) *The Philosophy of Social Explanation*. Oxford University Press, London, pp. 82-105.

Weitz, Richard (1993) 'Pursuing Military Security in Eastern Europe' in Keohane, Robert O., Joseph S. Nye & Stanley Hoffmann (eds.) *After the Cold War. International Institutions and State Strategies in Europe, 1989-1991*, Harvard University Press, Cambridge, USA, pp. 342-380.

Wendt, Alexander (1992) 'Anarchy is What States Make of It' *International Organization*, vol. 46 no. 2, pp. 391-425.

Wiberg, Håkon (1996) 'Adaptive Patterns and their Deep Roots: A European Overview' in Mouritzen, Hans, Ole Wæver & Håkon Wiberg *European Integration and National Adaptations - A Theoretical Inquiry*, Nova Science Publishers. Inc., New York, pp. 43-64.

Wilkenfeld, Jonathan et al. (1980) *Foreign Policy Behavior: The Interstate Behavior Analysis Model*, Sage, Beverly Hills.

Williams, Robin (1947) *The Reduction of Intergroup Tensions*. SSRC Bulletin 57, New York.

Wolfers, Arnold (1962) *Discord and Collaboration*, The John Hopkins Press, Baltimore.

Wæver, Ole, (1993) 'Europe: Stability and Responsibility' in *Internationales Umfeld, Sicherheitsinteressen und nationale Planung der Bundesrepublik*, Part C, vol.5, SWP, Ebenhausen, Germany, pp. 31-73.

Wæver, Ole (1995) 'Danish dilemmas: Foreign Policy Choices for the 21st Century', in Petersen, Nikolaj & Carsten Due-Nielsen (eds.) *Danish Foreign Policy 1968-1992*, DJØF, Copenhagen.

Wæver, Ole (1996) 'Power(s) and Polarity in Europe: 1989-1994 Patterns' in Mouritzen , Hans, Ole Wæver and Håkon Wiberg *European Integration and National Adaptations - A Theoretical Inquiry*, Nova Science Publishers. Inc., New York, pp. 29-42.

Young, Oran (1967) *The Intermediaries. Third Parties in International Crises*, Princeton University Press, New Jersey.

Zimmerman, William (1973) 'Issue-Area and Foreign-Policy Process', *American Political Science Review*, vol. 48 no. 4, pp. 1204-1212.

Index

References from Notes indicated by 'n' after page reference

activated vs. de-activated behaviour 44, 49
adaptation literature 24
alliance 3, 36, 54-5, 97-102
anarchy vs. hierarchy 7-10, 116-7
anti-holism/anti-historicism 148-9
anti-positivism/anti-inductivism 145-6
anti-psychologism/anti-reductionism 148-9
assumptions, view of 144

balance of threat theory 26-7
bandwagoning vs. balancing behaviour
    51-3, 97-102
bipolarity vs. post-bipolarity 1, 14, 28-9, 42
bottom-up perspective vs. top-down 2, 6,
    32, 139

comparative foreign policy 22-4
compatibility and consensus 24
complementarism vs. supplementarism 81-
    2, 151-3
constellation 36, 40-2, 43, 104, 108-11
consumers 1, 10
correspondence theory of truth 143
critical rationalism 141-50

differential impact 100-1
diffusion 63
distance, power and incentive waning with
    15, 33-4
    twin distance model 65-7, 78-9

ecological degradation 15
economic man 144
enduring rivalries 12-3
environment polarity 6, 34
    vs. regional polarity 38-42
    vs. systemic polarity 36-8
EU, as a power pole 38-9
    insider 40, 107-8
    outsider 41, 106-7
    would-be insider 40-1, 105-6
Europe
    integration 103-11
    power structure 38-42

value map 103-5
exile governments 10
explanation IX, 5, 32
    vs. description IX, 16
    levels of 5-7, 19-22, 81-2, 91, 147
        decision-making 6, 95-6
        domestic factors 6, 95-6
        salient environment 1, 2, 6, 31-6, 96
        subsystemic /regional 6, 21, 29
        systemic 6, 7, 10
external danger/internal cohesion-
        centralization 84-90
    anticipated reaction 85
    enforced 85
    spontaneous 85

falsificationism 149-50
foreign policy lessons 94-5, 101-3
fundamentalist opposition 87

game theory 13, 32, 87, 149
geo-politics 1, 24, 64-79, 97

high vs. low politics 116-23
holism 31

IGO 1, 3, 113-30
    actor properties 115-6
    as arena 115
    as state instrument 126-30
        articulator of guidelines 128
        face-saving device 127
        depository of legitimacy 127
        tool of binding 128
        tool of dependency spreading 128
    control-relax 113-21
    elasticity in state control 118
    fringe benefits 119-21
    general diplomacy 116, 119
    issue areas 115, 118
inductivism 23, 34, 146
inertia 12, 90, 92, 94-5
INGO 113
insider, EU 40, 107-8

interaction capacity 16
internal and external sources of foreign
    policy: their interplay 1, 3, 82-4, 95-6,
    97, 102-3, 111-2
  additive model 82, 92
  control-relax model 82-4, 91, 93-4, 102,
    104
  information model 92
international interdependence 14-6
international politics
  and foreign policy 5n, 6, 25, 153
  basic properties of IX, 1, 5
  fragmented 43, 149
international system 1, 7, 10, 16
IR discipline IX, 1, 5, 13, 21-2, 121, 138,
    142, 153-7
IR schools 129-30, 153-7
  IR realism 154-7

levels of analysis, literature on 19-22, 81-2

metaphysical realism 142-5
  vs. concept essentialism 144-5
  vs. relativism 143, 152
methodology 3, 142
mobile vs. non-mobile units 1, 5, 7-13, 90-
    2, 144
most-likely, least-likely cases 150

NATO issue-areas 125-6, 129
New Cold War 45-50
nomadic tribes 10
Nordic engagements vis à vis the Baltic
    countries 64-79

offensive vs. defensive power 44
organization theory 86, 117-8
outsider, EU 41, 106-7

party-system 8, 86
performative 144
permissive vs. efficient cause 104
pole vs. non-pole powers 14, 28
Popper, Karl R. 141-2, 145
pre-theory 2, 22-4, 43, 113

reductionism 2, 31-2, 148-9
regime, regime identity 32-3, 89
relativism 2, 143, 152

security, concept of 124-5, 145

shadow of the future 13
small state theorizing 23, 53, 63
soft sphere of influence 45
solidarity reward 89
SOP 12, 92
spatiality 8, 10, 11
status quo vs. revisionist power 100-1
symmetric vs. asymmetric relation to the
    poles 36, 43-4, 53-7

tension 43-4
theories of European integration
  control-relax vs. spill-over 132-4
  control-relax vs. calculated amalgamation
    134-6
theory 2, 85, 95
  and reality 2, 143

uncertainty avoidance 117-8
unintended consequences 129, 148-9
unit/system cleavage 8, 13, 28

virtue of simplicity 146-8

Waltz's 'Theory of International Politics'
    24-8
  and foreign policy 25, 153
  epistemology 147-9, 153, 157
  high vs. low politics 123
weapon-types 14-5
would-be insider, EU 40-1, 105-6